T0125211

Social Justice and the Indian Rope Trick

BY THE SAME AUTHOR

The State

Social Contract, Free Ride

Choice, Contract, Consent

Against Politics

Justice and Its Surroundings

Political Economy, Concisely

Political Philosophy, Clearly

Economic Sense and Nonsense

ANTHONY DE JASAY

Social Justice and the Indian Rope Trick

Anthony de Jasay

Edited by

HARTMUT KLIEMT

LIBERTY FUND

Indianapolis

This book is published by Liberty Fund, Inc.,
a foundation established to encourage study of the
ideal of a society of free and responsible individuals.

The cuneiform inscription that serves as our logo and
as the design motif for our endpapers is the earliest-known
written appearance of the word "freedom" (*amagi*), or "liberty."
It is taken from a clay document written about 2300 B.C.
in the Sumerian city-state of Lagash.

Compilation, preface, some articles, and index © 2015 by Liberty Fund, Inc.
Frontispiece by Lucinda Douglas-Menzies, reproduced by permission.

All rights reserved
Printed in the United States of America

C 10 9 8 7 6 5 4 3 2 1
P 10 9 8 7 6 5 4 3 2 1

Library of Congress Cataloging-in-Publication Data
De Jasay, Anthony, 1925–
[Essays. Selections.]
Social justice and the Indian rope trick /
Anthony de Jasay; edited by Hartmut Kliemt.
pages cm
([The collected papers of Anthony de Jasay])
Includes bibliographical references and index.
ISBN 978-0-86597-884-3 (hardcover: alk. paper)
ISBN 978-0-86597-885-0 (pbk.: alk. paper)
1. Social justice. 2. Economics—Sociological aspects.
I. Kliemt, Hartmut, 1949– II. Title.
HM671.D38 2015
303.3′72—dc23 2014016131

LIBERTY FUND, INC.
8335 Allison Pointe Trail, Suite 300
Indianapolis, Indiana 46250-1684

CONTENTS

PREFACE

This book is, for better or worse, unusual in more ways than one. It fits into a somewhat unusual personal history. I left my post of economist at Oxford more than half a century ago, ceased publishing learned papers, and disappeared from the intellectual scene. A quarter century later I resurfaced as a political philosopher with *The State,* my first and still the best-known of my books. It marked out my place at a distance from both classical and American liberalism, for reasons that will not be a secret to my readers. I never rejoined a university. I must have been swimming against the tide ever since, hardly progressing, though I hope that I have at least not been drifting with the mainstream. The present volume collects my writings on liberalism over the five years 2008 to 2012 and is a companion to the volume *Economic Sense and Nonsense,* my essays in political economy written over the same period.

The other and rather unusual feature of this book is its sharp focus on a vital but perilously ignored defect of modern political thought, namely the careless use, the misuse, and even the downright abuse of the language. The language directs the thought. Mainstream political thought from Bentham and J. S. Mill to the present is thickly polluted by intellectual fraud, if not altogether defined by it. The fraud is bona fide, for self-deception shelters it from the guilt of bad faith. It is not consciously trying to mislead or profit from passing off fraud for truth. It nonetheless deceives and nonetheless profits from it. The reason is that along the routes, corridors, and sewers of the subconscious, beliefs, including the values carried in our value judgments, are not independent of our existential interests. The argument in turn is not independent of our beliefs much as we might protest against the supposition of being led by ulterior motive. It takes iron discipline to keep matters of truth and falsity separate from matters of belief, and wishful thinking is, of course, often the source of belief.

Intellectual fraud, we are shown incisively, has invaded and come to dominate mainstream thought in shaping and twisting the meaning of some key concepts. Linguistic tricks are the powerful means of doing so, and are a central concern of the book. Linguistic tricks are the tools that shape concepts. The word "right" in such terms as "right to freedom" and "property rights" implicitly introduces a right-conferring society to which we owe such freedom and such property as it awards to us. The presumptions of freedom and of title are thus denied or ignored. References to social contracts or collective choice rules teach us, by implication, that one part of society, for example a minority, has agreed to submit to the decision of another part, for example a majority, of its own freewill and not in response to superior force. It has nothing to fear, since all decisions to which it must submit are constrained by a benign rule of collective choice or constitution. Should that rule prove to be less than benign as time passes, social choice theory prefers to look the other way.

The concept of equality put forward in the book is more complex than ordinary language makes it out to be. In its simplified form, it is regularly juxtaposed to inequality, with the former as an obviously superior feature of the state of the world. As the animals chant in George Orwell's *Animal Farm,* "Four legs good, Two legs bad." Relentless repetition goes a long way.

Plain misuse of language, however, is insufficient. Good is self-evidently better than bad and so is just better than unjust, but equal is not self-evidently better than unequal. A more powerful linguistic trick is needed to make it so. Social justice, reaching beyond ordinary justice and its rules, lacks rules of its own, and is empty of content like robes with no tangible body inside them. Linguistic usage effortlessly fills the empty clothes. Social injustice is automatically identified with some inequality, social justice with some equality. Equality is neither morally superior nor inferior to inequality, but it looks superior when it wears the robes of social justice. The word "social" only makes the robes more sumptuous and awesome. Social justice is thus established as a moral imperative, much as the Indian rope in the notorious trick is made to stand up skyward on its own.

"Just" being self-evidently superior to "unjust," the semantic trick of dressing up equality in the robes of social justice invests it with irresistible moral authority. Underlying the various themes of the present book is the general idea that the whole political order and the legitimacy of collective decisions have a further and perhaps less transparent linguistic trick as their sham ethical foundation. Most political theory is "contractarian" in a wide sense: it claims that there is a social contract of political obedience by which all agree in advance to submit to the decisions of some. Submission is uncoerced because it promotes some good. Contractarian theories are eagerly accepted, because they pander to the smug delusion, worthy of a rope trick, that individuals surrender their autonomy with their eyes wide open, rather than losing it by their own fault and then wishing that they had not. A central essay in the book, "Inadvertent Surrender," explores the way this is likely to come about. Rare is the resistance to it; as David Hume with his usual shrewd judgment tells us, obedience to government results not from positive consent but from acquiescence.

Anthony de Jasay

PART 1

Is Equal Superior?

1. EQUALITIES, THE CLAIMS OF SOCIAL JUSTICE, AND THE INDIAN ROPE TRICK

DIMENSIONS OF "EGALITARIANISM"

Word pairs like good-bad or just-unjust are hierarchical, the first word being self-evidently superior to the second. The pair equal-unequal is nonhierarchical, and equal is not self-evidently "better" than unequal. Equal shares in a distribution are usually understood as simple equality, "to each, the same." In relative equality, "to each, according to . . ." the share depends on some variable, e.g., work, and in compound equality, both the shares of a recipient and the whole distribution are a function of several variables, e.g., work, skill, seniority, responsibility, capital, etc. The distribution is deemed equal if it fits the characteristic function reasonably closely. These functions correspond to just deserts. Relative and compound shares must in an orderly pattern of distribution converge to the recipients' contributions to it. Such an orderly system may well appear as highly inegalitarian by the standard of simple equality. Failing the self-evident top rank of equality, many theories have been advanced to establish its superior value. These theories are either ethical or derived from putative facts of life (e.g., genetic selection). On scrutiny, their arguments are circular, irrational, or based on obsolete facts, and leave the moral or practical superiority of equal over unequal or vice versa at best undecided. Egalitarian thought, however, is triumphant as it tacitly identifies equality with social justice. As justice is superior to injustice, so social justice must be superior to social injustice. In this suggestion, there is a telling parallel with the famous Indian rope trick: the magician throws a rope up in the air; the rope stays upright and bears the weight of the person climbing up on it. Like the consumers of egalitarian theory, the spectators are convinced.

Previously unpublished; © 2015 by Liberty Fund, Inc.

The Meaning of "Social Justice"

What is social justice? One possible answer is that it is a value judgment passed on a state of affairs or an act. However, any number of value judgments can be passed on the same status quo or act. The same is true of ordinary justice, except that ordinary judgments that do not conform to the set of rules defining justice in a given social order would be thrown out as invalid and would not be enforced. Social judgments cannot be classed as valid or invalid because there is no set of rules of social justice, as distinct from ordinary justice, which they might obey or violate. Like other value judgments, judgments on social justice cannot validly claim to be true or false in the absence of rules defining what is socially unjust.

An attempt may be made to escape from this weakness of value judgments by limiting the range of judgments between two absolute extremes. One, Paradise, is as good as can be, and when judged as such, the judgment must have truth value. The other, Hell, is as bad as can be, and if judged as such, the judgment must have truth value. All real-life states of affairs can then be compared according to how close they are to the extremes. Such comparisons would, it is believed, bear a limited but undeniable truth value. This type of reasoning seems to underlie the position taken in modern utility theory in which one welfare judgment can indicate greater value than another because each has sufficient descriptive content to give it truth value. However, this escape route seems to be a cul-de-sac. Every value judgment has some descriptive content which must identify the subject being judged. This obvious fact does not suffice to transform all value judgments into statements of ascertainable facts. They remain subjective assessments that must modestly coexist with rival assessments.

Another possible answer is the one actually and almost instinctively taken by mainstream social justice theory. It cannot be satisfied with everyday language in which social justice is whatever is socially just, as fairness is whatever is fair. It must endow social justice at least with one rule to which it conforms and which injustice would be violating. That rule is equality in distributions. Albeit a coarse and unduly simple concept, it suffices to give social justice a status as a descriptive statement that can be true or false because equality and inequality are descriptive ideas. However, as will be argued presently, "equal" and "unequal" are not hierarchical, one is not self-evidently superior to the other; their ethical ranking or benign influence is decided by the merits of the case. Yet if equal were sometimes better than unequal and sometimes worse, then equality could not possibly serve as the rule filling social justice with a firm content. It becomes necessary to find at least a conclusive reason why equality must in all circumstances rank above inequality and thus give a lasting content to social justice.

The search for such a reason is critically surveyed in this essay.

Ultimately the solution of the search problem turns out to be to reverse the order of reasoning: since "equal" signifies socially just and "unequal" socially unjust, and just is superior to unjust, equality must rank above inequality. This is tantamount to the rope being thrown skyward and staying upright.

Several Equalities

This is an essay in the literal sense of the word. It is a *try,* exploring ways of finding answers to questions that are controversial and may even have no definitive answers. Perhaps most important, conventionally agreed answers imputed to them may turn out not to stand up to trial by elementary logic.

The questions revolve around several equalities and the imprecisely yet closely related notions of social justice. They deserve scrutiny not so much for their intrinsic intellectual interest, which is hardly outstanding, but rather due to their being a subject of the most intense preoccupation by society as a whole and serving as a prime mover of political action.

We speak of equal liberties, equal rights, equal opportunities, and of course equal shares in the goods and bads that life and the rules it follows keep distributing among us. Some of these equalities are conceptually loose and open to rival interpretations. Equal opportunity is one such. Some are just confirmations and indeed redundant reiterations of what more basic concepts imply and more basic rules require anyway.

In my view, equal liberties and equal rights fall in this category. They will not be touched upon here. Most of the arguments that follow will deal with the equality of shares to recipients in a distribution of desirable (or undesirable) entities, such as money, property, work, options, or obligations. The distribution must be quantitatively specified and the set of recipients clearly circumscribed. The entities distributed must have a common denominator and must be sufficiently divisible.

In simple equality, each recipient gets the same share; "to each, the same." In relative equality, the share of each depends on some variable defining who he is and what he is doing in that capacity. For instance, the recipient may be a hospital nurse and her share will depend only on how many hours she has worked in a week. The dependent variable, her pay, may be a linear function of the independent variable, her hours, or a nonlinear, i.e., degressive or progressive one. Relative equality responds to the order "To each, according to. . . ." In compound equality the share of each, as well as the whole distribution, depends on several variables in various ways. The hospital nurse is probably paid according to her qualifications, her seniority, and the hours she works. The hospital, a distributive institution, has a payroll that depends on an even larger number of independent variables including the status of each class of its staff, their qualifications, the responsibilities they bear, the amount of work they do, and perhaps several other, less obvious ones. All such multivariable distributions can conveniently be called "compound." The economy of a country is the most eloquent example of a compound equality. The compound equality demonstrates that an aggregate displaying a decidedly unequal, and perhaps quite disorderly, pattern distribution in fact conceals within itself a number of simple, relative, and compound equalities that may account for most or all of the aggregate.

Equality in the ordinary language of common and also of political discourse is almost exclusively intended to mean simple equality. The literature of political philosophy likewise tends to ignore relative or functional equality and focuses on simple equality, as if simple equality were alone politically relevant and ethically normal, as if its status as the norm were established.

Some of the arguments against simple equality also speak against relative equality, but not all do. Separate treatment of the two should mitigate the risk of confusion from this source.

SIMPLE EQUALITY: TO EACH THE SAME

Is Equality Self-evidently Superior?

Good-bad, satisfactory-unsatisfactory, abundant-scarce, healthy-sick, strong-weak, adequate-insufficient, true-false, honest-dishonest, etc., etc., . . .

In each of these pairs, the first member ranks self-evidently above the second. This is so in both individual and social preference orderings (if one allows that the latter sort exist in some sensible format), as well as in evaluations by the "impartial observer." If morality is to be thought of as independent of preferences, one should also say that the first members of these pairs are morally superior to the second. Self-evidence makes all further argument in support of the ranking redundant and out of place. It is simply idiotic to ask whether "good" is better than "bad," "adequate" better than "insufficient."

Is equal–unequal a pair like the ones above? Asked why "equal" is better few people would regard the question as simply idiotic. Clearly, it is not, though some of the answers offered may well be thought to be so. Many ordinary people would confidently affirm that equal is *just,* unequal *unjust,* as if *this* were self-evident, hence an answer neither requiring nor leaving room for argument. The stratagem of simply identifying the non-self-evidently better "equal" with the self-evidently better "just" and leaving the matter at that is hardly adopted knowingly, but is all the more effective for that, as are many other beliefs whose only support is that they are sincerely held.

Many egalitarian academics spoil this effect to some extent by constructing theories of justice that are mostly elaborate arguments meant to serve as bridges from equality to justice or vice versa. But attempts to prove a metaphysical belief do not serve them well.

What egalitarian theories demonstrate is that "equality," not being self-evidently better than "inequality," needs *reasons* for so regarding it. Arguments are ever contentious, always potential victims of counter-arguments. Arguments that are devoid of empirical propositions, much as they may attract our sympathy or our disdain, remain indecisive to the end, rolling along in a debate that only boredom and a sense of irrelevance could terminate. Overcoming this fatality would require some miraculous demonstration that "equal" is self-evidently better than "unequal."

None of this is generally recognized. Current usage in both everyday speech and academic discourse persists in employing "inequality" as a pejorative word, unwittingly implying self-evidence of the underlying evaluation. Those who so employ it would on reflection quite likely concede that it is silly to put "unequal" on a par with "bad," but sloppy thinking, passion, and habit bar the way to reflection.

Thus, the accelerated globalization of the last quarter century is commented upon by many reputable economists as a prime cause of unprecedented growth in world output (which it is), but also as a cause of the shift of factor shares in favor of capital and to the detriment of labor, of rising inequality between rich and poor (which is contestable but which the skillful deployment of statistics can "show to be true"). Greater output is good, greater inequality of its distribution is bad, and globalization is good or bad according to the balance between the good and the bad which it brings about. The dialectic exercise rests upon an unspoken affirmation of self-evidence; one does not have to argue that inequality is bad. It is enough to call it by its name. Since the point is simply subsumed and not at all labored, it is widely accepted as something that goes without saying.

Recent and current debates about proposals for the reform of higher education take the same dialectic form. The proposals promise positive effects on university government, the dropout rate, staff selection and incentives, grade inflation, and so forth. They have the promotion of excellence, hence of inequality, as one of their objectives, and so are invariably diagnosed as enhancing inequality and condemned. No one feels the need to ask why "inequality" in this context, or indeed in any other, is treated as an obvious, recognized negative whose badness goes without saying. Other examples of the question-begging practice of using "inequality" as a pejorative word accepted as such by all could be listed but do not seem to me to make a strong case any stronger.

The debate between equality and inequality could be decisively ended in favor of equality only if the argument were to show that the *reason why* the latter is preferable or in some other sense superior is itself a self-evident one. It would not suffice to argue, as has been done, that because factors making for inequality are "morally arbitrary," they should have no weight in deciding a distribution that would be just because unanimously agreed to be equal. In this chain of reasoning, the equal distribution is just because it is agreed, but the *reason why* this happens depends on the arbitrary assumption that inequality is the product of moral arbitrariness and that fair-minded parties to a negotiated distribution would refuse to take into account morally arbitrary factors. There is no self-evident reason why all should be fair-minded, or why, if they were, moral arbitrariness (rather than immorality, a breach of self-evident moral rules) should in their eyes disqualify a distribution and move them to choose another.

Moral arbitrariness seems to be rejected on one of two grounds. One is that arbitrariness is ipso facto bad. With a little good will, this could be accepted as a plausible axiom. The other ground is that it is unfair, a judgment reached by defining "fairness" as the property of a distribution purged of moral arbitrariness (achieved by John Rawls in creating his Original Position by the device of the veil of ignorance). This reasoning is patently circular. Other, less convoluted arguments also tend to try and establish the superiority of equality on some metaphysical ground. Accordingly, they can always be countered by other metaphysical arguments without either side creating a presumption let alone a conclusion in its favor. However, efforts both with and without recourse to some prior reason continue to assert the dominant rank of equality.

Do Ethical Judgments Favor Equality?

Failing self-evidence of equality's superior rank, the second line of its defense is metaphysical. An ethical judgment must be made about the ranking of distributions. Though such judgments have no claim to be true or false and a judgment favoring equality is no more valid than one favoring inequality, there are well-known arguments in favor of the former that aim to render the egalitarian judgment more plausible than its opposite.

A radically simple version of these is the blank assertion that equality is fair, inequality unfair. Since "fairness" lacks an accepted definition independent of equality itself, the statement "equality is fair" will under pressure become "equality is equal" and be rightly dismissed as an ill-concealed tautology.

Equality is fair because it is not morally arbitrary, moral arbitrariness being unfair—the defense of the ethical judgment—is reduced to a mere circularity. A more traditional approach to influencing ethical judgment in favor of equality is broadly utilitarian. It is of two kinds. One appeals to the perceptions of the judge as he observes the "pain and pleasure" the recipients in a distribution receive from it. He is relying on empathy. The other kind appeals to the preferences of the recipients themselves, the judge having no role except to take note of what the recipients declare they prefer. In the first kind of persuasive approach, the judge, an Impartial Observer, finds that rich people derive less of whatever they seek from a unit of the good distributed than do poor people. The entity they all seek, whether identified as satisfaction, happiness, or well-being, is to be unified and labeled as "utility," a metaphysical construct. The fact that the rich man derives less utility from one unit of the good than the poor man may mean that the utility of the rich rises by a smaller proportion of itself than that of the poor; the former may have his utility increased by one millionth, the poor by one tenth. However, much as this may influence the judge in favor of changing the distribution in favor of the poor, he cannot honestly say that the one-millionth increase in the rich man's "utils" is smaller than the one-tenth rise in the "utils" of the poor man, let alone by how much. The two cannot be added to or subtracted from each other. Neither level nor difference comparisons make sense unless the "utils" of the two persons are commensurate. They are rendered commensurate by, in effect, assuming that they are, for as Bentham once ruefully remarked, otherwise "all practical reasoning is at an end" and the Impartial Observer cannot say that one distribution is better than another without giving up his impartiality.

Formally (though not in substance) the argument can be sustained by imagining a version of utility that is commensurate, permitting "practical reasoning," i.e., both level and difference comparisons. Commensurate utility may exist only in the imagination but, rather like the winged horse or the magic potion, it enables a seductive story to be told to its foreordained end. Given all these somewhat extravagant assumptions, the judge judges that by depriving a person having a large share in the distribution of one unit of the good being shared out, and giving it to one having a smaller share, the total of commensurate "utils" in the distribution will rise. All rich-to-poor transfers will have this effect. Obviously, the aggregate "utils" will reach a maximum when no inequalities in shares remain and no further "util"-enhancing transfers can be made.

In the other type of ethical judgment, it is the participants who by their behavior demonstrate that they want an equal distribution. However—an important and usually only implicit proviso—they must want this unanimously unless a separate ethical judgment decrees that minorities agree to submit to majorities without threat of force.

The recipients would all decline a bet on the even chance of winning and losing a sum of money. In a thought experiment, they are confronted with an equal probability of living in any one of the "social slots"—"slots" for the rich, the poor, and the in-between—that make up a society. Since they decline even-chance bets, they also decline an even chance of a rich and a poor "slot," and judge that they prefer a society of equality where all the "slots" are the same.

In a slightly different version starting with an unequal distribution, those with a share below the mean prefer a redistribution which raises their share toward the mean. Counterintuitively, those with a share above the mean also want the same redistribution, pushing down their share toward the mean. The putative reason is that they see the future shrouded in a "veil of uncertainty" and believe (oddly enough, we must remark) that without a redistribution, their future share would be as likely to be below as above the mean.

It is perhaps worth noting that it seems irrational for the rich to believe that stepping behind the "veil of uncertainty" they will have lost awareness of all the endowments, legacies, talents, and characters that have made them rich to start with, and have no better than an even chance of staying rich. However, this result would seem less irrational, or at any rate less implausible, if it was supposed that beyond the veil people are in the "Original Position" and ignore the endowments they possess. The scenario would be even more painfully contrived, but at least seem more sensible.

Without sometimes only implicit reliance on extreme assumptions—commensurate "utils," universally declining marginal utility, very acute empathy, universal "risk aversion," veils of uncertainty and ignorance—the notion that ethical judgments are bound to lean in favor of equal utility is untenable. We simply cannot prejudge and predict which way logically less ill-supported judgments would lean.

Does Evolution Select Equality?

It is sometimes suggested that a propensity for equal sharing is implanted in man's genes. It disposes us to seek equal distributions not only when equality is reached by getting something from others, the commonplace motive for calling for equality, but also when we must give them something of ours. There is an underlying supposition that in the natural course of events we take turns taking and giving so that gains and losses tend to even out, and that the result is better for all concerned than if they did not share and share alike.

The propensity to share is supposed to be "hardwired" into human nature and got there by genetic selection when man was a hunter-gatherer wandering about in very small groups. In this existence, the availability of food depended on a constant, the prowess and experience of the man who was hunting the aurochs and of the woman who was finding the berries and the mushrooms, and a number of variables including luck, the weather, the abundance or scarcity of game, fish and vegetal edibles, the state of health of the hunters and the gatherers, and perhaps others less obvious and harder to think of. As the variables changed, the group would pass through phases of satiety and hunger in a largely unpredictable sequence. In conditions of scarcity, the dictates of genetic survival would induce the dominant male or matriarch to distribute the available food unequally, by favoring the next of kin over the more distant kin. In fact, the distant kin might have to be allowed to die if not actually aided to die.

Equal distribution might, however, prevail over the unequal one if there was a tacit understanding with other groups that were hunting and gathering within walking distance of the first group. The groups that happened to have surplus food would invite the ones deficient in food to a feast, a "potlatch," or let them have food in whatever other manner would save the faces of the recipients. Theoretically at least, share-and-share-alike, a pooling of resources, and their distribution in equal portions could be the result. Pooling would not help the participants if all they had to pool was their common misery because, for instance, all would be equally afflicted by the same disease, the same drought, the same dearth of game. It is not unlikely that this would be the case some of the time, the misery of one being positively correlated with the misery of others in a wide geographical area. Negative correlation, on the other hand, would produce a strong case for equal sharing that, by evening out the peaks and troughs of the food supply, would promote genetic survival for those who practiced it. One might make the case for equality even stronger by recognizing that since the equal sharing of hunger and misery is not obviously worse than suffering them individually in isolation, pooling and sharing is never worse than nonsharing and often it is better, i.e., Pareto-superior. It works like a convention that it is in everybody's interest that everybody else should conform to and, given that sanctions against free riding evolve and are firm enough, it is in the interest of everybody to conform to.

Lest these facts-of-life arguments for equality should seem overwhelming, let us recall that while there are many variables that make the food supply of the hunter-gatherer group gyrate up and down both absolutely and sometimes relative to other groups, there is a constant—the personal qualities, skills, and experience of the group's leaders—that will always give them more food than other groups with less clever hunters and mushroom pickers. It could well be that in a prehistoric, fairly simple context this factor, favoring unequal distribution, is swamped by those favoring an equal one. However, the factor in question will inevitably crop up again and play a role in more modern contexts.

In the modern context, the share-and-share-alike policy is represented by the metaphor of "society is a mutual insurance association" suggesting that ups and downs in individual distributive shares even out by egalitarian redistribution, the "ups" paying the premium and the "downs" getting the insurance payouts. However, income and wealth in modern society are much less stochastic than game and berries feeding the hunter-gatherers. The "ups" mostly remain up over a lifetime or even through generations, and the "downs" mostly remain down. Much the same people pay the premiums all the time and seldom or never get the insurance payments. The metaphor of society being a mutual insurance association is egregiously misleading. There is no earthly reason why the share-and-share-alike policy imputed to the ups should be helpful for their survival and reproduction, and why it should be selected by genetic evolution.

If anything, the share-and-share-alike policy promotes the survival and reproduction of the downs, the needy and also the less able whose distributive share is increased by what they get from the "ups," the well endowed, keen and shrewd.

It has been asserted that share-and-share-alike having been the practice to aid survivors of the hunter-gatherer existence over a very long period, in distant prehistory it got "hardwired" into our genes and remains a fact of life and a permanent standard of behavior into the modern age. Assessing this claim is not easy, the less so as egalitarianism in distribution is far from being a universal standard of behavior today even if it was really one in prehistory. One may reflect, however, that since hunter-gatherer bands in each other's vicinity must have been subjected to much the same periods of abundance and scarcity, and that abundance and scarcity for everyone at the same time do not offer scope for mutual insurance, the incentive to share as between two or more bands must have been limited. There was almost certainly an incentive to share within the band, but maybe for different reasons than usually imagined. The cleverest hunter (or subgroup) killed more game than the others and might have wished to take all or more than an equal share of the meat for himself and his closest kin. However, if he killed the aurochs, he could not conveniently appropriate the surplus meat; preserving it was difficult, and carrying it along as the band wandered on was even more so. Sharing it was better than wasting it.

This technological bias in favor of sharing disappeared little by little as wandering mostly ceased and sedentary agriculture replaced hunting-gathering. Serfs and farmers tilling more land than the neighbor and being cleverer at it harvested more and kept the surplus grain in clay jars till the next harvest, to the sole benefit of their own and their closest kin. Save-and-store as a policy for survival and reproduction dominated share-and-share-alike. It continued to do so through history to our age. It is hard to credit that our genetic makeup has failed to adapt to this, remains stuck with behavior that suited conditions in the dismal prehistory but serves no evolutionary purpose today, if it is not to assist the survival of the unfit. If they see which way it points, defenders of redistribution as a manifestation of the evolutionary process might wish to moderate their advocacy.

RELATIVE AND COMPOUND EQUALITY

The battlefield of egalitarian theory is almost completely confined to simple equality, the response to the command "To each, the same." It seeks to show that this ought to be the case by virtue of the superiority of equal over unequal sharing. Since "equal" is not self-evidently superior to "unequal" the way "good" is superior to "bad" or "ample" is to "scarce," reasons must be found that adequately support the assumption of the superiority of the one over the other. Ethical judgments and the conditions of genetic evolution are proposed as such reasons. They are implausible and can hardly be accepted as adequate; the question of why the assumption should be allowed to stand remains devoid of an answer.

The natures of relative and of compound equality are diametrically opposed. A distribution where each share responds to the command "To each, according to" some variable (relative equality) or to a set of variables (compound equality) is what it is for some reason. Its form is ascertainable by observation. Its theory is a generalization of descriptive features, grounded in findings that are not, or hardly at all, in dispute. Open questions are confined to distributive features of a status quo that escape the command of "To each, according to . . ."

The crucial ascertainable fact that renders the theory descriptive is the set of spontaneously emerging[1] conventional rules functioning as the rules of justice and thus as purely voluntary constraints of conduct.

Just Deserts

At least a minimum of attention should be paid to why a given person's share in a distribution depends wholly or mostly on a particular variable.

Tales meant to educate the public in what the storyteller is pleased to call "distributive justice" habitually take a thoroughly bizarre form.

1. See "The Limits of Conventional Morality and Justice," in this paper, pp. 19–27.

A cake is said to be waiting for a decision on how it shall be "sliced." Silence reigns about the why and how the cake came to be available as well as about who is entitled to slice it. Nor does it transpire who is to get a slice. The play seems to revolve only about whether some slices should be greater than others, though the final answer is invariably that they should all be equal if only because no sufficient reason intrudes into the tale for admitting that some should get bigger slices than others. A necessary preliminary to disposing of this bizarre story is to realize that all justice is distributive. Its rules partly if not wholly determine benefits and burdens, rewards and punishments, assets and liabilities. "Distributive justice" is either no more than a mere pleonasm or a misuse of language for no ulterior motive, or else a veiled insinuation that beyond ordinary justice there is another distinct sort of justice with a separate competence in matters of distribution. Should we innocently inquire about where this specialized justice comes from and what its rules may be, we would learn that it is all about compelling moral intuition that right-thinking persons can be persuaded to make their own.

Thinking about the tale of the cake should show at once that there is no pure distribution problem insulated from the rules of justice that it could shut out from the solution. J. S. Mill tried to do this by declaring that production obeys the laws of economics, but distribution is for society to decide. Amartya Sen tried to do it in his *The Idea of Justice* when discussing who of three children should get a flute made by one of them, without showing how a flute belongs to nobody and is available for adjudication without first taking it away from somebody. The present author tried to expose the peculiar bias of this approach by calling an essay of his on the subject "Slicing the Cake That Nobody Baked." In fact, it is unconscionable to discourse about the destiny of the cake without recognizing that those who baked it have a prior claim on deciding who may slice it and who shall get which slice. This claim is theirs until they cede it.

When the cake is prepared, the baker-entrepreneur acquires contributions to its making, buying labor from willing-seller workers and capital from willing-lender or willing-investor capitalists. If he runs his enterprise the most efficient way, he will buy both labor and capital up to the point where their respective marginal contributions to the cake just match their prices. It is when the price they obtain equals their marginal product that they will have obtained their just deserts.

With exchanges agreed without fear or favor and with mutually advantageous conventions ensuring the respect of contracts, just deserts may reasonably be held to be established by the rules of justice.

Admittedly, we cannot find by direct observation whether the prices received by workers and capitalists so equal the marginal products. The world being less than perfectly ordered, there may well be "backer-entrepreneurs" who pay less than the marginal contribution they get, and we may in fact suspect some of doing that. With the willing buyer–willing seller relation preserved, this is not unjust even if labor or capital do not get their just deserts. However, if the "bakery" in question remains successful and its success does not provoke more intense competition, we infer that just-deserts factor prices may not be far off. If rivals do enter the cake business, just-deserts factor prices may be established quite rapidly. A distribution makes sense to us if we accept the conjecture that the share of each is based on a tendency for it to converge toward the marginal product the recipient of the share contributes to the total to be distributed. It is thus that the share of each ultimately approaches his or her just deserts.

Hidden Equality

Distribution is made to recipients by distributive institutions which dispose of the good or bad to be shared out according to some pattern. They dispose of a given quantity of the good or bad either directly or by administering rules within which the recipients arrange the distribution among themselves. The share of each person may be the same as that of every other; this is the case of simple equality, a context that helps to focus attention on the status of equality as a principle and the widely made claim that it is morally superior to inequality. An alternative pattern, relative equality, allocates shares relative to who the recipient is or what he does; when this variable is present to different degrees in the being or doing of different individuals, their distributive share would vary accordingly in proportion (Aristotlean equality) or in some nonlinear yet regular fashion. Finally, when the pattern is made up of individual shares that may depend on several variables to different extents, we are confronted with compound equality as a characteristic of some or all of the total distribution.

With the school canteen being the distributing institution, each child is given the same meal regardless of who they are and how they conduct themselves. Simple equality prevails. When the institution is the school, each child gets more or less education according to his or her collaboration with the teacher (though if he wished to pursue the matter, we might say that the quantity or intensity of his collaboration was itself a variable of his intelligence, willingness to work, manners, etc.). With the institution understood as embracing an entire country's educational system, different shares go to different students depending on a much larger set of variables than the ones determining the shares of children in a single classroom or single school. In addition, however, some of the goods and bads are also distributed to different teachers according to their qualifications and perhaps also according to their zeal or the results they obtain. Nor must administrators, examiners, and anyone else who from near or far contributes to education be left out.

Compound equality can at least in principle be detected by submitting the pattern of distribution to regression analysis with respect to each independent variable that we suspect of having an influence on the pattern. Taking the payroll of an industrial corporation as a more apt example than the school system, we may find that one part of the payroll is closely correlated with the hours worked by one class of employees, with productivity and skill having more influence on more specialized parts of the work force, as did length of service. Graduation from business schools of widely different prestige might be decisive for the pay of young but not of middle-aged executives, and so forth. A large number of correlations between independent variables and distributive shares accruing to parts of the work force could account for a significant proportion of the total distribution that would thus reveal itself as a sum of simple and relative equalities. The residue could either be accepted as indeterminate and chaotic, or if too large, be pursued further by regression analysis with respect to less obviously relevant variables.

Observed from the outside, a pattern with a reasonably high degree of compound equality must look glaringly inegalitarian and would qualify as such even by less impressionistic, objective measures such as a fairly high Gini coefficient. However, the surface inequality would in effect be hiding a highly structured web of simple, relative, and compound partial equalities, where each reason for getting a distributive share duly generated the share to the recipient in some orderly relation to itself.

Such a compound equality, however it may look in its disguise of inequality, cannot persuasively be criticized on grounds of its not being equal, but rather, and perhaps only, on the ground that we disagree with the reasons that explain it. In other words, the critic agrees that the distribution is grounded on reasons, but he disapproves of the latter. Teachers should not get more pay for better results, young executives should not profit from having had the opportunity to buy a business education, and senior army officers in wartime should have no power to order other ranks to take risks that they do not themselves take. Critique of a pattern whose various constituent equalities have various reasons thus ultimately ends as a demand for simple equality without any saving grace that would justify treating it as some final principle that must be accepted as an axiom.

THE LIMITS OF CONVENTIONAL MORALITY AND JUSTICE

Morality in Coordination Equilibria

Supporters of the primacy of simple equality over inequality often omit to take account of the fact that translating equality into an actual state of affairs brings it into a head-on clash with individual autonomy. At least some persons in society would not voluntarily give up some of their freedom and goods for the sake of equality, and would have to be subjected to the threat of force. If one person is not entitled to do this to another, ten or ten million are not entitled either. If autonomy is a first principle, it must not be subordinated to equality. The latter cannot have the rank of first principle if a conflict of the two is to be avoided. The obverse is also true.

The conflict would become less clear-cut if it were the case that individual autonomy must be submitted to collective choice if social order is to be created and maintained. This is a superficial and mistaken supposition.

Each person finds some advantage in coordinating his or her behavior with the behavior he or she anticipates that others will adopt when anticipating his or her behavior. If either party makes a mistake in anticipating the response another party will make to his behavior, surprise and disappointment ensue and the "players'" behavior is ill coordinated. In real life, coordination is facilitated if each player, instead of being matched randomly with others in successive replays, is mainly matched with members of a specific group to which he belongs as the inhabitant of a locality, the member of a church or association, a worker in an enterprise, or one of a peer group. Experience of repeated interactions obviously heightens the predictability of responses to one's behavior. As predictability becomes more complete and the scale of the group whose members behave mostly predictably widens, we may say that a convention has emerged.

The convention is an equilibrium. In an equilibrium no member of an interacting group can benefit by unilaterally changing his strategy if others do not change theirs (the "strategy" of each being the set of responses to various hypothetical moves of the other).

Like Hobbes who had no trust in "covenants without the sword," mainstream opinion has little belief in the self-enforcing capacity of conventional rules. It is a widely held position that for spontaneous conventions to be obeyed, a specialized enforcing agent like the state is required, though it is often left unexplained why the agent should act in the best interests of the principals. This view about self-enforcement is essentially due to the failure to appreciate that individuals are confronted by conventions in a repeated, continuous manner and their evaluation of the pay-offs available to them is influenced by the "shadow of the future."

To avoid a frequent misunderstanding a very small handful of special conventions should be excluded from the argument that follows. These conventions, e.g., the rules of the road, language, weights and measures and money, require no enforcement, because deviation from them is dominated by conformity to them. Driving on the wrong side of the road is self-mutilating and we need not pursue the matter any further. Our lack of further interest is strengthened by the conventions in question having no moral dimension.

The main body of conventions that is of concern tends to be morally offensive and appears to offer temptation to the individual to behave badly. Any such convention implies the free-rider option of not obeying it. Everyone prefers everyone else to obey it while he is left to profit from the good behavior of the others. These others naturally seek to deter resort to the free-rider option. This may be done by a range of facts, acts, and signals. The direct victim of another's disobedience to the convention, as well as his close associates, may retaliate. Others not directly harmed by the disobedience may put out warning signals, threatening retaliation against any future disobedience that weakens the fruitfulness of the convention. Since any such enforcing action exerts an influence on future obedience, it improves a long series of future payoffs flowing from the convention.

The standard objection to this argument is that while everyone prefers everyone else to assume the cost of enforcement everyone would rather not assume it himself. In other words, the free-rider problem of the convention is replicated in the enforcement of the convention. The present author used to hold that this objection can be overcome by the formation of satellite conventions to back up the conventions themselves. In the satellite, the enforcement itself would be enforced. Obviously such an approach is tantamount to starting off an infinite regress, a sure sign that the approach is unfruitful.

The author now takes the view that the enforcement of the enforcement is an integral part of the convention and need not be treated as a separate problem calling for a separate solution. The plain man's view of the whole matter should best be that rational individuals will find it worthwhile to find enforcing solutions to make worthwhile conventions work. It is perhaps not lacking in respect to say that this view is not far removed from that foundational element of game theory, the Folk Theorem.

On one side we would put conventions that *facilitate* the business of life, such as the rules of the road, the use of a common language, the adoption of weights and measures or of paper money. They are nonconflictual, are morally indifferent, require no enforcing sanctions, and do not protect against deliberate wrongdoing. These conventions are not moral in the ordinary sense. The reason for holding this view and distinguishing them from moral conventions is that they do not involve wrongdoing or harm to others as a strategic option that is rejected in moral play. Adhering to the coordination equilibrium and resisting the temptation of doing wrong involves no moral merit. Driving on the right is not a moral act. Square dealing is arguably one, even though it is the best equilibrium available. On the other side of the divide we find virtually every other convention.

Some social philosophers seem to think only of the first type of self-enforcement and ignore the second. Reserving the term "convention" for the first case of self-enforcement, they are greatly underrating the role and significance of processes of self-enforcement. A possible reason is that they are programmed to think of revenge and retaliation employing force as itself an illicit, deviant response unless carried out by the state that has "the monopoly of the legitimate use of force." However, in an ongoing game the punishment of deviant behavior can be an equilibrium move *in the repeated game* even if punishment is costly for the retaliating individual. To incur that cost is rational for the individual since, in case of not punishing, retaliation for not punishing is to be expected, and so on.

Typically there will be an infinity of—often quite complicated—equilibria in which individuals will punish in view of expected future rewards or punishments. A convention may emerge as one from the indefinite number of equilibria, and equilibrium selection becomes an integral part of the evolution of morality.

Consider the example of cheating and its social antidote, the convention of square dealing or honest conduct as a coordination game. Counterfactually, one could imagine a "parametric" society where everyone acts as he pleases without anticipating reactions of others. There would be no "strategic" interaction of adjusting behavior to the expected behavior of others. Each player would be cheating as often as he saw fit without regard to how this would affect the cheating of others. Despite the satisfaction each might find in yielding to his inclination without restraining it, such a world would be "nasty, brutish, solitary" and perhaps above all "poor" for all too obvious reasons. Anyone who shed the parametric blindness and saw the strategic interaction where others might react to whether he cheated or dealt honestly would be facing two alternatives. In one, others he happened to deal with would cheat as much as before or perhaps worse than before (free riders) if his honest dealing had made him a more attractive victim (a sucker). This outcome, then, would be "weakly worse" than if he had never tried to give up cheating. The other, more cheerful alternative is that his honest dealing would elicit honest dealing by the other party, who by repaying honesty with honesty expects to improve the probability that at their next encounter the first party will be tempted to act honestly once again. Both realize that if this were to happen frequently over several future encounters, the outcome for both would be superior to what either the sucker or the free-rider outcome could yield.

Unrestrained cheating by everyone all the time would, then, be the lower bound and honest conduct by everyone all the time the upper bound of a zone of possible equilibria. This is the familiar solution of the repeated prisoners' dilemma game. Despite somewhat esoteric qualifications and reservations game theorists like to surround it with, the theorem is conclusively confirmed in real-life business where the typical behavior pattern is square dealing in response to the same by most parties ("honesty pays"), mixed with a sprinkling of rather sporadic cheating that necessitates precautions and increases dealing costs, but does not impair the equilibrium found somewhere between the lower and the upper bound of coordinated behavior.

What raises the equilibrium above the lower bound and some way toward the upper one might be called selfish self-denial. The word "selfish" is used to signify that the motivation is entirely self-interested, so that any good or bad effect on another player is purely an externality. The self-denying player renounces "passion" for "reason" (to use Humean language). The self-denying person does what he does for reasons of his own, but his action can appear fully compatible with a plausible level of rationality if he is assumed to believe there is sufficient probability that the responses of others to his self-denial will be selfishly self-denying, too. In saying so, we are not claiming that a convention of coordination evolves because the relevant probabilities make it seem profitable, but that since the convention has evolved and is proving profitable, it must be compatible with the probabilities a calculating player would impute to it. Random actions springing from haywire impulses or mere copycat conformism independent of the expected rewards of morally coordinated self-denial could explain neither the breadth of the interactions conventions govern nor the longevity of the most crucial ones.

An upward shift of the chosen coordination equilibrium requires that both (or all) players abandon their current strategy and shift their degree of cooperation upward in the same proportion; in the game of "honest conduct," they must all cheat less frequently. In noncooperative play with sequential moves, the first mover must quit the safety of equilibrium and move upward (cheat less) without any assurance that the other player(s) will respond by similarly moving upward and cheating less, establishing a new, higher equilibrium. If they do not do so, "sticking his neck out" will put the first player in the "sucker" position, to be exploited by "free riders."

We know from anthropology that inviting others to step up their degree of cooperation by "sticking their necks out" must have proved a good (payoff-enhancing) strategy. If it had been bad (payoff-reducing), the emergence and survival of coordinating conventions would be very hard to explain. It would have to be credited to supernatural commands or to some eccentric motive like masochism. There is no point in entertaining such possibilities.

Moral Conventions

The crucial conventions, without which human coexistence in normal circumstances would not be conceivable, are the *conventions against torts* which prohibit killing and serious bodily harm as well as their threat except in the course of enforcing the convention that establishes property and reserves for the owner its use and disposal (implying the barring of dispossession, trespass, theft, and fraud), as well as the convention of keeping promises. A little reflection can show that these conventions, unless narrowly and literally interpreted, contain within themselves protections and interdictions that political discourse likes to enumerate separately as achievements of the social contract or the constitution. It is difficult, for instance, forcibly to violate people's liberty and "basic rights" without infringing the conventions against torts and particularly against serious harm or its threat to integrity of person and property. It is hardly necessary to affirm a person's liberty peacefully to pursue his harmless purposes or to speak his mind if stopping him or gagging him would involve a breach of some of the conventions against torts. Imputing the existence of conventional rules to the need to protect people's hypothetical "rights" to life, limb, property, safe pursuit of peaceful purposes, and free speech poses the question of where these rights come from or who had the power to award them and erect the rules to protect them. It is not hard to see why no such unanswerable questions arise when, instead of *rights* that seem to have fallen from heaven, we seek the origin of conventions in the elementary *wrongs* that individuals can reduce or avoid by reciprocally coordinating their conduct with one another. Other than in the case of choosing one side of the road what is a tort is not arbitrary. Even if what is treated as a tort is conventionally fixed, there is a reason in human interest and nature that "suggests" it.

Less crucial than the conventions against torts are those against *nuisances* and *incivilities*. Their nature and functions are explained by their names. They are important for tolerable life, but not important for the subject of the present essay, and they will be undeservedly but expediently left on one side. "Conventions" henceforth will mean those against torts.

Conventional rules can aspire to the rank of moral rules. This proposition will be taken as read here. A further proposition would hold that only conventionally arising rules deserve the rank of moral rules. I think this proposition is excessive but nevertheless worth entertaining with careful qualifications.

Two conditions seem to me necessary for recognizing that a rule is a moral rule. One is that obedience to the rule should not, or not only, be the result of some probability of a feared sanction, but also of self-denial.

The second necessary condition is that the goodness of the consequences of observing the rules should be self-evident. This is the case, not simply because coordination yields a greater game-sum than noncoordination and a high degree of coordination yields more than a low one. Such an outcome, though prima facie good, is not self-evidently so, for it leaves open the possibility that in the noncoordinated disequilibrium, some players gain a large share of a small game sum at the expense of other players, while obeying the rule together with everyone else would earn them a smaller gain even though the total game sum was larger. This possibility is remote, for it supposes that where nobody plays by the same, or any, rules, a player can go on expecting to gain much at the expense of the others without the game disintegrating. Where everybody plays "free rider," no free ride is possible because nobody is left to free-ride on. Nevertheless, the prima facie case that the coordination equilibrium is self-evidently good because it raises the available payoff is not cast-iron if it must rely on plausibility. However, in its place, we may say instead that the rule is self-evidently good because no player prefers that any other player should fail to obey it. This must be true of any sane player, for even the one who plans to live by defrauding or stealing from others will prefer that others should not defraud or steal from him. In this sense the moral rule of the coordination equilibrium is a unanimity rule that everybody wishes everybody else to obey.

It will surely not escape the reader's attention that the moral rule system whose genesis is the spontaneous acceptance of coordination has a strength not shared by any other known moral rule system: it depends on no putative authority such as divine revelation or the mandate nonunanimously bestowed on a legislature to generate lay law.

The self-evident goodness of conventionally reached moral laws has a very direct bearing on the place and rank of equality. Many of these rules pre-empt solution of distribution problems, leaving no choice between equality and inequality. The rules protecting the person and his or her property are the conspicuous example of such preemption favoring inequality. Regarding equality and inequality as available alternatives in these areas is to admit that moral rules born of coordination equilibria may be treated as subordinated and may be violated for the sake of some other good. This may or may not be a tenable position. What seems to be important for the time being is to make the rule violation involved quite explicit, something the egalitarian literature does not do with the outspokenness that the subject demands.

Not all moral rules can be traced to coordination equilibria, though those that can are the easiest to explain in the traditional language of payoff maximization. In this tradition, we say that a higher payoff is preferred to a lower one and the preferred is chosen, or more directly (since preference may not be revealed otherwise than by the choice itself) that the higher payoff is chosen. It makes sense to say that self-denial is selfish, to the extent that it is instrumental in securing the higher payoff for oneself without regard to any adverse effect on others.

However, while it seems to me right to say that all moral rules are self-denying, it would be wrong to assert that the self-denial is always a means to payoff maximization. Saying this would make sense if all actual choices were preferred ones and "preferred" was synonymous with "higher payoff." There is no reason why the words in question should have to have this meaning. If they were so understood, every choice would be payoff maximizing and maximization would be reduced to a boring tautology.

Shaking off the tautology lends comfort to an undisguised division between moral rules best understood if they are ascribed to selfishness and those best explained by selflessness. The latter would be recognized as the demands of virtue, while the former may well not be.

The moral rules that are likely to spring to mind when selfless self-denial is considered as the principal kind of motive for obeying them are the sense of duty, self-respect (honor), respect for others, and charity. Others might make a different and probably longer list. For our purpose, it suffices to recognize the existence of a class of selfless rules and note that obedience to them is likely to be totally voluntary in the sense of not depending on any sanction, personal, social, or other.

THE INDIAN ROPE TRICK

Fair Words

"Fair" is a word that, significantly enough, exists only in English and has not even remote foreign equivalents; it has an unparalleled diversity of meanings, most of which are vague and uncertain; and despite the prominent role it plays in the language of private arrangements and public affairs, it has ever remained a rather formless, pliable notion that has never hardened into a precise concept, nor was much attempt made by philosophers so to harden it. It was always tacitly assumed that when we say "fair" we all know what we mean and we all mean much the same thing.

A fair man takes no advantage of another, plays by the rules, sees both sides of an argument, and has other virtues too numerous to list; he is also blond. A fair woman is pretty or at least good-looking, for fairies are nice. In a fair deal, neither party gains noticeably more than the other. Fair shares are what people get out of a fair deal. A fair amount is not too much, but just adequate, and a fair way off is neither very far nor very near. Fair weather is weather we like and a fair wind is what a ship needs to sail both fast and pleasantly. Having a fair go is attempting something under reasonable conditions, and getting a fair go is to have such conditions rather than very favorable ones. "Fair average quality," or "faq," is how Australian wheat is marketed, as opposed to Manitoba wheat that is graded. Fair day's work is what can reasonably be expected of you but that does not break your back. In fair competition, your rival is not placed better than you and does not press you unduly. In sum, fair is nice.

In contrast to the equal-unequal pair of opposites that does not imply the ranking of one over the other, the pair fair-unfair, of course, is hierarchical and fair is self-evidently on top. The pattern of distribution in a fair society needs no other justification than that it is the pattern that a fair society generates. Beyond believing that it would be nice, people have only the vaguest and often mutually contradictory ideas of what it would take for society to be fair.

Political philosophy has not been of much help in this regard. There is no proposed set of sufficient conditions, let alone an agreed set, that would identify a society as a fair one.

Tentative moves to find a definition have admittedly been made. One, proposed by Ken Binmore, notes that in games with multiple coordination equilibria, the fair one will actually be chosen. However, we do not know whether it is chosen because it is fair or fair because it is chosen. Clearly, fairness needs to be independently identified to fill this void.

A more ambitious approach, commented upon in another context above, is that of John Rawls. Absence of moral arbitrariness (obtained by the "veil of ignorance" blotting out awareness of all the advantages and handicaps that would influence distributive shares if they were not blotted out) makes them opt for a fair distribution; but the reason why advantages and handicaps must be blotted out, namely their moral arbitrariness, is none other than that the latter is not fair.

The notion of fairness is both purely defined and admits of a multiplicity of meanings that lead in a variety of directions that all have a common element: they all attract the mind by reasonableness, sweetness, and light.

Despite its circular, if not downright tautological character, fairness powerfully assists egalitarian discourse. In effect, it is a tame derivative of egalitarianism with all the merciless nature of the latter removed. Egalitarianism threatens all who have incomes or wealth above the mean, and deprives many of what they believe to be their rightful property. Fairness does not menace, since any redistribution that it requires is supposed to be the result of purely voluntary agreement.

A rough-and-ready way to cut through its circularity might be to postulate that any distribution is fair that depends only on people's own efforts and the advantages they have earned by their efforts. It would therefore be independent of three major influences: inherited property, talent, and luck. Shares would depend on property accumulated by the recipient's own endeavors and abstinence, his acquired skill, his effort at deploying it, and some insurance mechanism sheltering him from both good and bad luck.

However, the objections to such a (rather "Dworkinian") definition of fairness are crushing. Depriving persons of their inherited property and its fruits yet allowing them the property they acquire for themselves cuts across the spontaneous conventional rules of justice that, in Hume's words, secure "the stability of possession, its translation by consent, and the performance of promises"[2] between parents and children no less than between other consenting parties. In addition, it would wreak havoc with capital accumulation, for the lifetime saving of a rational father who could not "translate" it to his son would be zero. Capital accumulation may have nothing to do with fairness, but a society that failed to accumulate would soon have survival rather than fairness to worry about. Insulating talents from the determinants of shares would be undermined by the notorious subjectivity of drawing a line between raw talent as a genetic endowment and the will and effort it takes to develop and cultivate it. Skill, too, is likely to be the joint

2. David Hume, *A Treatise of Human Nature,* reprinted from the original edition in three volumes and edited, with an analytical index, by L. A. Selby-Bigge, M.A. (Oxford: Clarendon Press, 1896), sect. 8: Of the source of allegiance. From http://oll.libertyfund.org/title/342/55231/608062.

product of talent, learning, and experience, concluding the occasions for learning and experience that may not be the fruits of a person's own efforts. Finally, the effect of good and bad luck on one's distributive share is hardly a matter of blind fate, for it must depend at least to some extent on how the person positions himself or herself so as to face one probability distribution of possible future events rather than another. Insulating the person from both deliberately accepted and totally unforeseen risk by insurance raises complicated questions of moral hazard and others that are too tangled to be unraveled in the framework of this essay. The whole question of transforming society into a mutual insurance association is too vast and too treacherous to be more than hinted at here.

If it were not for these objections to the idea of fairness as a distribution depending only on personal merit and effort, the result would be inconclusive and its reality difficult to ascertain by observation. Pursuing the matter seems simply not worthwhile. Fairness is not a fruitful subject for social theory.

For what it is worth, we may note that an imaginary pattern of distribution putatively shaped by merit and effort would display a large measure of simple inequality concealing relative and compound equalities, a measure that may be no smaller than the apparent simple inequality of any other distribution not constrained by the exclusion of all the variables that we may wish to brand as unfair. Fairness beyond fair words and vague aspiration to niceness cannot be affirmed to exist as a properly formed concept. Still less can it be expected to serve as a support for, let alone to take the place of, simple equality.

Social Justice at the End

It is perhaps pardonable to remind the reader at this juncture that obtaining and preserving tenure of state power and enforcing collective choices within a society that is seldom wholly homogenous and never unanimous in sentiment and interests are problems that arise continually and require indefinitely repeated political action. Such action is part intimidation assuring acquiescence and part bribe buying consent, with the proportions between the two varying widely according to cultural and historical circumstances. Intimidation tends to predominate when the ultimate holders of state power rely on the support of a well-organized and cohesive minority, well separated from the majority by ethnic origin or class and exercising authority strengthened by habit and precedent. The support of this minority is typically cemented by privileges and wealth conceded to them at the expense of the majority. In one word, the tenure of power mainly by intimidation reduces to redistribution from poor to rich.

The tenure of power mainly by way of bribe is symmetrically the opposite of tenure by intimidation. On this type of structure, the holders of state power purchase the consent of the majority by transferring to it income taken from the minority and rendering it public services partly financed by the latter. In this type of state structure, redistribution is mostly if not always wholly from rich to poor.

For a variety of reasons, some good and some less so, in recent history consent bought from the majority with resources taken from the minority has come to predominate and has in fact been more and more explicitly formalized by the adoption of majority voting as the standard collective choice rule. Moreover, the tenure of state power has to be regained on its expiration in the face of competition by rivals, involving a periodic bidding contest for majority support.

The scope of rich-to-poor redistribution is naturally limited by the extent of inequality of distribution prior to the redistribution. As long as the mean income in a society is above the median, there is a majority of potential winners from redistribution that pulls the mean down toward the median, i.e., that reduces inequality. It is tempting to think that redistribution thus eats its own scope, with no potential left for finding a winning majority once the mean income descends to the level of the median and simple equality is established.

In fact, if account is taken of the passing of time, it becomes clear that simple inequality is continually reproduced as relative and compound inequalities, since differences in property, marginal productivity, and effort among individuals persist. Redistribution, too, can therefore equally persist without necessarily exhausting its own scope. Exhaustion of a quite different origin and kind may well occur due to the burden of taxation and the temptation to burden future generations with state debt that a regime of persistent heavy redistribution may bring about, but this is at worst a highly probable contingency rather than a necessary corollary of majority rule.

Permanent rich-to-poor redistribution as a corollary of majority rule has a wholly decisive impact upon egalitarian theory. It moves it far away from the aura of inconclusiveness, from the lack of self-evidence that this essay has been arguing.

Redistribution serving to gain and retain political power by bribing the majority is opportunistic and cynical. It breaches the principle of distributive shares corresponding to just deserts. It violates the spontaneous conventional rules of justice, including the ancient ingrained sense of property, of mine-and-thine. All this odium is swept away by the linguistic masterstroke of calling redistribution the doing of social justice, just as the work of the judiciary authority is called the doing of justice. As justice is superior to injustice and it is desirable that the former should redress the latter, so must social justice by symmetry be superior to social injustice and must redress it. The linguistic masterstroke is in no way conscious and conspiratorial. It has not been cunningly invented by a clever egalitarian theorist. But the dressing up of egalitarianism in the clothes of justice has completely changed its status. It is plain to see that social justice must be superior to social injustice.

In days past, crowds in Inshamudheen Delhi and Padmaraj have seen with their naked eye the Indian magician throwing a length of rope up in the air and his boy assistant merrily climbing it until he disappeared in the height. Nobody could dispute the evidence of his own eyes and doubt the firmness of the rope's upright stand. Social justice is performing the same miraculous trick as the Indian rope. Few of us seem to disbelieve it.

2. RANKING WORLDS BY WORDS
A CASE FOR INEQUALITY

A few years ago, a powerful head of state was chided in private for his statist economic policies being in flagrant contradiction with his free-market convictions. Ever shrewd, he replied: "Everybody wants to go to heaven, but nobody wants to die." Professional politicians certainly do not; acting on unpopular principles is their rare luxury, but avoiding political suicide is a dire necessity.

Václav Klaus has come closer than almost any contemporary statesman to emancipating himself from this dismal rule. He is of the almost extinct species, the conviction politician. I first met him during the time when the Soviet Union was breaking into pieces, and I have taken much pleasure in following his career ever since. We have had few occasions to exchange views, but I have been an admiring, distant witness of his actions in the service of his country and the liberal principles we share.

HIERARCHICAL ADJECTIVES

1a. "Recent economic developments in East and South Asia and Latin America have accelerated the rise of average incomes, *but* have increased inequality."

"University reform in France may enhance achievements in higher education, *but* it is bound to increase inequality."

Were it not for the *but* asking to be remarked on by being in italics, such sentences might well have passed most readers without alerting them to the part of their meaning that is left implicit. Higher incomes and improved education are presented as good changes in the

From *Today's World and Václav Klaus, Festschrift in Honor of Václav Klaus, President of the Czech Republic* (Prague: Nakladatelství FRAGMENT, s.r.o., 2011), 155–62. Reprinted by permission.

state of the world, greater inequalities as bad changes, the one being as self-evident as the other. A world where some characteristics, e.g., the incomes of different people, are equal is self-evidently superior to another world that is identical in all respects except for the characteristics in question, e.g., incomes that are unequal. The words "equal" and "unequal" rank them in a peremptory manner that assumes self-evidence, rendering any supporting argument redundant and out of place. The innocuous little word "but" accomplishes this feat. Were it replaced by "and," the sentences above would leave the question of a more equal world being superior or inferior to a more unequal one, or being simply incommensurate with it, scrupulously open.

One may add that the use of the "but" is legitimate only if the question of the superiority of equal over unequal in any relevant respect has been decisively settled. If such is not the case, employing "unequal" as self-evidently signifying a bad thing that offsets some good thing, is at best sloppy and naive, at worse a sleight of hand of doubtful honesty.

The power of words to establish a hierarchy between worlds will be looked at a little more systematically in Section 1b.

1b. *Good-bad, beautiful-ugly, useful-useless, clever-dumb, adequate-inadequate, just-unjust.*

Big-small, long-short, loose-tight, heavy-light, soft-hard, equal-unequal.

As it transpires from the example of the two sets of pairs of contrasting adjectives above, some of these pairs establish hierarchical ranks between the characteristics of worlds to which they are *ceteris paribus* applied, while others do not. The second of the two sets does not settle rank; if two worlds differ only in one having a characteristic that is long and the other one that is short, whether one is superior to the other depends on the particular characteristic in question. Long life-expectancy may outrank short life-expectancy, but long working hours may be less agreeable than short ones: without identifying which characteristic is meant, the issue cannot be decisively settled. At any rate, however, if such words determine cet. par. rankings of states of the world, they do so based on the merits of cases.

The first set of pairs is obviously of a radically different kind. A world where something is good is self-evidently better than one where it is bad. Demanding an explicit axiom stating that good is better than bad would be foolishly pompous.

PLAUSIBILITY

The reader will have noted that the word pair "equal-unequal" figures in our second set where one member of the pair is not self-evidently better, preferable, or in some other relevant respect superior to the other. Putting the pair in the first set, as if it were in some way beyond dispute, and it went without saying that equal ranks (morally and materially) above unequal, while in harmony with much current practice, would be begging the question. Failure to recognize that it did would, as we have argued above, be naive or sloppy, if not a dubiously honest maneuver.

A formally less objectionable procedure is explicitly to adopt some axiom that raises equality above inequality. It is noteworthy to mention how rarely this is done and how general has become the practice of proceeding as if the superiority of equality were a matter settled a long way back which now stands unshakably against all objections.

However, the axiomatic treatment is safe only if we accept the axiom regardless of what it asserts as long as it suffices to make a deduction formally complete. If, however, the axiom must also be plausible, it leaves the argument for equality seriously vulnerable.

Egalitarian discourse employs a number of fundamental abstractions which, if they were convincing, would also serve to make an equality axiom plausible. Three seem to me to stand out.

One such is that God has created all men equal. Except for identical twins, this is manifestly untrue as a matter of empirical fact, for six billion men and women are unequal in innumerable characteristics. As a nonfactual moral proposition, the phrase has no particular content and entails no consequence. An alternative foundation that would entail a normative consequence is that all human beings are worthy of equal respect. Introspection tells the present author that he holds some people in much higher respect than others, that he even holds some in contempt, that he regards these inequalities as richly deserved and that most of his fellow men distribute their respect in a similarly unequal fashion. Finally, it has become conventional wisdom among egalitarians that unequal distributions of good (and presumably also of bad) things that are due to unequal endowments are unfair, because the endowments themselves are "morally arbitrary." Since, however, there exists no known moral rule proscribing endowments such as talents and character, nor one that would admit them but only if they were equal among individuals, consequences of endowments are morally neutral. Neutrality is not arbitrariness; the latter is pejorative, the former is not. It would indeed be "morally arbitrary" to condemn the distributional consequences of different endowments as morally arbitrary.

In sum, neither of these frequently invoked general arguments contributes much, if anything, to making an equality axiom look sufficiently plausible. This may well be the, albeit subconscious, reason why such an axiom is rarely, if ever, postulated—much as it would help to establish some logical structure for egalitarian theory. On the other hand, lacking an axiomatic fastening, the advocate of equality as self-evidently superior to inequality needs the power of the Indian fakir who throws a rope up in the air and proceeds to climb up on it.

EQUAL EQUALS JUST

The linguistic version of the Indian rope trick has been effectively performed under our credulous eyes in the last half-century or so. Its ever easier acceptance by the practitioners of political discourse and their public roughly coincided with the retreat of Benthamite utilitarianism and the advance of Kantian rightism and its popular outgrowth, the idea that justice entails "equal" liberty and a qualified equality of the distribution of "primary goods." "Equal" liberty has subsequently been expanded to "equal capability" to do, which must imply that in a just society, individuals' feasible sets are equal.

These abstract propositions of rightism are affirmations that gain credibility and more or less subconscious acceptance by virtue of relentless repetition and also of the favorable disposition of the public. This disposition may have various origins, one of which is no doubt the residual effect of several religions. However, a sufficient explanation is, simply, that "existence determines consciousness" and most people will readily believe affirmations that favor their interests. Anyone whose income, wealth, or status is below the mean can expect to gain in a world where the relevant distributions are more equal; hence he will be well disposed to agree that more equal distributions are more just or, in pure binary terms, that equal is just, unequal is unjust.

The essence of the Indian rope trick in ethics, then, is surreptitiously to identify "equal"—which may or may not be superior to "unequal" depending on the merits of the case—with "just," which is self-evidently superior to "unjust" and never mind the case in point. The identification is rendered less brazen by appending "social" to "just." Social justice is said to be a sort of justice, but as it is not defined *what* sort, we have no other choice than either to accept it without further argument or dismiss it because it deserves no argument.

"Social" justice may be a fudge and its use to promote equality as self-evidently superior to inequality may be a linguistic version of the Indian rope trick, but it has gained for itself a vast public. Not all of this public is endowed with sharp critical faculties, and not all who are well endowed feel like exercising their faculties to oppose social justice, still less to be seen opposing it. However, if it were tried, how should critical opposition proceed?

JUDGING CASES ON THEIR MERITS

Pairs of such contrasting words as "big" and "small" or "hot" and "cold" do not place one word above another the way such pairs as "good" or "bad," "just" or "unjust" do. They may promote or demote depending on the merits of the case. Hot signifies a better world if it refers to an oven, a greenhouse, or breaking news, while cold is superior when it describes an icebox, drinking water, or dispassionate reason. The words "equal" and "unequal" likewise change their roles according to cases, rather than one always conferring superiority and the other inferiority. When the two sides of a face are equal, the symmetry contributes to an impression of beauty that pleases. Isaiah Berlin in fact believed that the appreciation of equality could be explained by the love of symmetry. We need not share this diagnosis, but we may note that while symmetry is superior in some respects, asymmetry is better in others. The two sides of an automobile had better be symmetric, but the front and the rear had best not be.

In some of these respects, there is a unanimously admitted superiority of one over the other. The two front tires of a motor car ought to have the same pressure, while between the front and the rear pair of tires unequal pressure is better. In some cases, the agreed superiority of the equal over the unequal, or vice versa, is due to a misunderstanding. It is widely and in some sense rightly held that equality before the law characterizes a better world than either randomness of judgments or systematic bias in favor of or against defined parties. The misunderstanding lies in mistaking the rule that rules must be applied without exceptions, for equality before the law. Randomness would obviously violate this rule and would be a bad thing. On the other hand, there may be a system of laws providing privileges and exemptions for defined persons or classes and perhaps also discriminating against others, which may strike some observers as equitable and others as outrageous (the tax code of most countries is an example), but whose faithful application must pass as equality before the law.

The real battlefield where the two rivals must fight it out on the merits of cases is, of course, distributional equality. The latter refers to the way a divisible good or bad is divided among the members of a defined group. They may share it equally; simple equality is "to each the same"; e.g. all employees of a corporation from chairman to doorman are paid the same. Compound equality is perfected "to each, according to . . ." where the share of each person is the dependent variable in some function whose arguments may be time spent, effort, result, seniority, status, etc. Obviously, there are distributions that are unequal in both the simple and the compound sense, being at least partly determined by prior ownership, parametric market forces, or ad hoc bargains and often also by sheer luck. These are true inequalities in everybody's book.

If, as we argue, there is no self-evident superiority of equality, equal and unequal distributions must be ranked by the merits of cases and the merits must be instrumental.

The instrumental merits of a distribution are of two main types. One argues as if wealth or income were the main criterion of a good distribution, the other as if happiness were the real object of it.

It is usually accepted that inequality serves wealth or income both because of its incentive effects and because it favors the accumulation of capital, hence the demand for labor, so that both the rich and the poor ultimately get richer. By the same argument, an equal distribution perpetuates poverty. Against this view, egalitarians could object that some very unequal distributions in feudal Europe or Central America have led to stagnation rather than capital accumulation, and that economic growth is promoted more by historical and cultural factors than by an unequal distribution.

The other main type of the on-the-merits argument is made by "happiness economics." Inequalities provoke envy, competitive stress, anxiety, while equality brings appeasement and nonrivalry. These claims are supported by people's oral declarations and as such may be disbelieved. Objective data, too, are often cited in support. In societies with more unequal distributions, health, life expectancy, and school results are worse than in egalitarian ones. This phenomenon may have two explanations: one, that some people are richer than others, and the other, that some people are poor. Happiness economics cannot tell which explanation is right and which distribution makes for more happiness.

In fine, however, all the "for" and "against" arguments alluded to above weigh more in some cases and less in others. If judgments about the ranking of types of worlds could be made on the mere strength of the words "equal" and "unequal," rather than on the merits of cases, one would simply have to accept a reminder that social justice is just, because this is self-evident in its name. The Indian rope trick would have to be swallowed.

A DRAW AND A PRESUMPTION

It would be underrating the tenacity of systemic partisans to expect every debate about the ranking of equality and inequality in a particular case to be decided one way or the other. In some, it is hopeless to search for the knockdown argument, and the last word keeps receding into the indefinite future. With the best efforts of socialists and liberals producing an intellectual draw, what is to be done?

There is a handful of very important contests where, pending a last word that may or may not be forthcoming, good sense and logic impose an interim solution which allocates the burden of proof to one party and, until it is discharged, imposes a presumption of what the case is. The presumption of innocence is one of these; the presumption of good title to possessions is another. Perhaps the most important and least well understood is the presumption of freedom. More precisely, it is the freedom of a defendant to engage in conduct a plaintiff claims is inadmissible and ought to be prohibited or circumscribed. The presumption prevails and the freedom is perpetuated if the plaintiff fails conclusively to prove that it ought not. In political systems where collective choice enjoys ultimate authority, its decision to forbid a given conduct may override the presumption of freedom, but does not invalidate its logic.

A draw between arguments for equality and inequality also generates a presumption that is partly, though not wholly, analogous with the three classic ones mentioned above. The burden of proof need not be assigned to one of the parties to the debate. In a draw, neither party could discharge it. Failing conclusive argument that it ought to be changed, the world of the status quo prevails. If the latter is in relevant respects unequal, it continues to be unequal. If, by virtue of past and present egalitarian policies, it is in relevant respects equal, and the draw leaves it undecided whether this is good or bad, superior or inferior to its alternative, the presumption calls for its being left well alone. There is no presumption in favor of continuing the maintenance of equalities by continuous redistribution and the other related measures meant to prevent inequalities from arising again.

3. AGAINST POVERTY AND THE MISUSE OF LANGUAGE THAT HELPS TO PERPETUATE IT

INTRODUCTION

Spoken and written statements reveal part of what we have in mind in order to inform and persuade others. They can be designed, or may just happen, to implant in others beliefs and preferences they might otherwise not have. Language, then, is a remarkably subtle tool in the hands both of the manipulators who abuse it by design and the unconscious who do not perceive the work it is doing. Consider two statements where what Gilbert Ryle called "systematically misleading" language is employed. One fails in its object, the other succeeds.

1. "She is a pretty girl, but she has deep blue eyes." The first part of the sentence praises the girl, but the "but" that separates the two parts signifies that having deep blue eyes detracts from the girl's prettiness. This is clearly nonsense; there is no earthly reason why we should believe that the girl would look prettier still if her eyes were not deep blue. The "but" separating the two parts of the statement is either a mistake or a failed attempt to persuade us that the girl would be prettier if her eyes were not blue. If the "but" were replaced by "and," the second part of the statement would simply add information to the first part without trying, and failing, to offset or altogether negate it.

2. "Economic growth in Southeast Asia has accelerated in the last decade, but inequality in income and wealth has also increased markedly." The writer of this sentence is telling us that the first half is good news and the second bad, the latter offsetting some or all of the goodness of the former. What is perhaps more subtly misleading is that the badness of the second half is implanted in the sentence as a matter of self-evidence. The "but" tells it all; instead of an argument that in-

From *Economics, Politics, Philosophy, and the Arts: Essays in Honor of H.S.H. Prince Philipp of Liechtenstein,* ed. Kurt R. Leube (Triesen, Liechtenstein: Van Eck Verlag, 2011), 15–19. Reprinted by permission of Kurt R. Leube.

equality is in some decisive sense a bad thing, it simply treats it as if it went without saying, a matter of self-evident truth agreed by all and demanding no supporting reason. The linguistically neutral separation of the two parts of the statement should be by an "and" rather than the "but," for the "and" would not prejudge an issue that is very far from being self-evident. The present essay seeks to show some of the reasons why it is not.

Statement 2 is a classic case of the type of systematically misleading language poured forth in crescendo by professional intellectuals, politicians as well as churchmen since the latter part of the eighteenth century. Because it panders to the primary instincts of many ordinary men and to the immediately palpable interests of a majority of them, treating equality of income and status as self-evidently superior to their inequality in some decisive sense has, in our time, become second nature and unnoticed and unchallenged. Most of those who, without noticing their own slothfulness of thought, employ the crucial "but," sincerely believe that by promoting equality as an undisputed good, they are serving the cause of the poor. It strikes the present author as tragic-comic that the opposite is almost certainly the case.

LANGUAGE THAT PREPARES THE GROUND

Demanding distributional equality implies the forcible alteration of the (unequal) status quo. Losers and gainers are thus created and this complicates matters of ethics even if the self-evident superiority of equality were conceded and even if such a concession were not purely arbitrary, ex gratia. It is presumably for this reason that egalitarian theorists are often driven to reason about how manna fallen from heaven should be shared, or which of those children should be given the flute that belongs to nobody.

John Stuart Mill, than whom few have done more to dilute liberal thought by sheer well intentioned efforts to broaden it, has circumvented the problem of the status quo by emptying it. In the status quo that precedes the distribution he postulates (i.e., that to be decided by society), there is no distribution, hence nothing to be forcibly undone.

In his *Principles of Political Economy* (1848), Book I deals with Production and Book II with Distribution, implying by such language that these are two distinct events in a sequence. First the cake is baked, then it is sliced and shared out. He teaches that production is subjected to the laws of economics, while distribution of the produce is for society to decide. In fact, however, the distinction and the two-step sequence are facile linguistic fictions, misrepresenting reality, though convenient in preparing the ground for egalitarian theory.

It is not good manners to quote oneself, but I do it all the same because I can think of no more concise way of putting the matter than in my essay "Parrot Talk": ". . . production and distribution are simultaneous aspects of the economic process. Output is distributed while it is produced. Wage earners get some of it as wages in exchange for their effort; owners of capital get some of it as interest and rent in exchange for past saving. Entrepreneurs get the residual as profit in exchange for organization and risk bearing. By the time the cake is 'baked,' it is also sliced and those who played a part in baking it have all got their slices. No distributive decision is missing, left over for 'society' to take."[1]

What "society" can and typically does do is to use the state's coercive powers, taking possession by direct and indirect taxation of bits of everybody's slices. Thus, it can modify the primary distribution by a secondary redistribution. However, if you believe that doing this does not impinge on the "baking of the cake" that is taking place at the same time, you will believe anything.

In any case, the metaphor of first baking the cake and then sharing it, insulated by the language employed from antecedents as well as from the all too likely consequences of sharing the cake by "social" choice, clears the ground for pure egalitarian theories that are both nonconsequentialist (because consequences of the egalitarian distribution are implicitly denied) and counterfactual (because the ground is in fact not clear, but cluttered with facts from the status quo ante and from the diversity of the actors on the scene). The cake gets baked for no apparent reason and then gets shared out equally, for no one has a better claim to a share than the next person. There are of course

1. First published in *Cato Journal* 28, no. 1 (Winter 2008), and reprinted in *Collected Papers of Anthony de Jasay, Political Philosophy, Clearly,* Indianapolis: Liberty Fund, 2010. German translation "Papageiengeschwätz" in *Liberale Vernunft. Soziale Verwirrung, Studien zur Wirtschafts- und Gesellschaftsordnung,* Vol. V, ECAEF (Vaduz, Fla.).

a number of theories of just distribution that thrive in the ground so conveniently prepared. In the present essay, I propose to steer clear of them, and limit my arguments, in what I hope is a more hardheaded manner, to matters that are ascertainable in connecting equality and poverty.

THE PRESUMPTION OF INEQUALITY

I use "presumption" in the sense that we must presume something to be the case until a sufficient reason is shown that it is not. It is practically unfeasible and in some cases logically impossible to show that something is the case, but short of the metaphysical domain it may be possible to show that it is not; the burden of proof against the presumption lies on the challenger. Freedom, innocence, and good title to possession are the best-known presumptions. The presumption of inequality could be added to them with equal logic. We may conjecture, and may expect to find, that a distribution of goods (incomes, riches, status) will be unequal unless sufficient reason making it equal is found. The basis of the presumption is that unlike in the pious rhetoric where "all men are created equal," in the real world all men are created unequal to varying degrees. Each person can be more or less fully described in terms of some of his innumerable characteristics. Even if all persons had a handful of the same characteristics and had them to the same degree—a difficult condition to fulfill—each person would have a vast number of other characteristics in which he differed from others either altogether or at least in degree. Inequality in some respects and to some degree is clearly the general case. Differences are rooted in the genetic heritage and the upbringing of individuals, which makes a population of equals hardly conceivable.

In a society where goods and services are produced and voluntarily exchanged, all characteristics of a person may be relevant to his relative success to obtain what he seeks, and some characteristics are obviously very relevant. Energy, strength of will, talent, brains, perseverance, training, and what are called the "social skills" predestine people to material success if their luck is no worse than random. With the passage of time, initial success and initial inequality of distribution become cumulative in a variety of ways. The well to do tend to have well-to-do friends and more rewarding opportunities for reciprocal give-and-take. They can shed unproductive tasks, discharging them on hired help, and concentrate on their own comparative advantages. They at least can, even if they do not always do it, devote more attention to the upbringing of their children to improve their chances of becoming successful, too. Last but not least, they can save a higher proportion of their income than the unsuccessful. Accumulation of capital to a greater extent secures them additional income; this advantage is cumulative and can be transmitted. Thus, failing sufficient reason to the contrary, we may expect distributions in general, and the distribution of the national income in particular, to be unequal. The inequality may have a tendency to increase with time, though probably at a diminishing marginal rate due to the effect of capital accumulation upon the demand for labor and wage incomes. Changes in technology may vary periodically from capital-saving to labor-saving or vice versa, and influence the part of inequality that is due to unequal ownership of capital. However, compared to the force of differential personal endowments, these effects are likely to be second-order.

Taxation of income and wealth does, of course, weaken the presumption of inequality, though no mere fiscal measures could ever achieve complete equality, if only because the harsher the measure, the more reckless and vigorous noncompliance and evasion are likely to become. However, this, too, is secondary to our main theme, in which equality and inequality may be matters of degree and not binary alternatives.

SUPPRESSED INEQUALITY, STAGNANT EQUALITY

Suppressing inequality involves costs, which are likely to be more than linear increasing function of the degree of equality aimed at (and a fortiori the one actually achieved).

Three kinds of cost are involved. One, fairly easily ascertainable, is spent on enforcement in a broad sense, ranging from the record-keeping taxable subjects must engage in, to detective work to catch evaders and litigation to resolve disputed cases. The second and prima facie much greater cost is also ascertainable, though only in a probabilistic sense. It is the forgone capital accumulation due to a given income being distributed more equally. The very rich, even the ones who spend ostentatiously, consume only a smallish fraction of their income and save the bulk of it. The well to do save a somewhat smaller proportion of it, while the needy may not be able to save at all or may even dissave. Thus, capital accumulation out of a given national income will be lower as income distribution becomes more equal. The third element of cost is likely to be vastly higher than the first two, but this is not ascertainable and must remain a matter of educated conjecture. Hundreds of books and thousands of editorials have discussed it, often in an axe-grinding, tendentious fashion. Suffice it to say here that excepting the poll tax, any taxation, including the "flat tax," worsens the marginal rate of transformation of effort into net income. This tends to reduce productive effort in the broadest sense, including enterprise, initiative as well as routine daily grind. One exception is the person whose fixed commitments do not permit any reduction of net income and who must increase effort as effort becomes less rewarding. Cases of such positive (perverse) elasticity of the supply of effort no doubt exist, but negative (normal) elasticity is likely to be more prevalent and more voluminous in its effect on total national income. To the extent that forgone capital accumulation, as its name tells us, is cumulative, it depresses national income not once, but progressively. In other words, it depresses the rate of growth.

In sum, significantly suppressing the inequality of distribution that arises spontaneously from the diversity of genetic and acquired endowments has a cost whose total is made up of both actual and of opportunity costs and may be difficult to quantify precisely, but looks like it will be heavy.

It may also be called the maintenance cost of a significant measure of equality in distribution, and this name is definitely more telling. What does it buy? In particular, what does it buy for the poor, whom we must suppose to be its principal beneficiary?

The poor face two alternatives, though it may not really be they who choose and who deserve the blame due for making the wrong choice. The gap between the mean and the median of the national income is narrowed by progressive taxation; the "juice" squeezed from the gap is pumped into the below-median region by a variety of means including more public goods and services and more welfare entitlements and this is accompanied by much "churning." The upshot is a modest and immediate rise in the real income of the needy destined to stagnate at that level in perpetuity, or grow only slowly. The other alternative is that inequality is left intact; the poor stay as poor today as they were yesterday, but find themselves tomorrow on a growth path much steeper than what the more egalitarian distribution would be able to produce. If capital is at all productive, not to speak of enterprise and innovation, a decade of continuing inequality may quite possibly double the per capita income of the poor. Other ways of fighting poverty, if restricted to the means a stagnant or only barely growing national income can spare, look like puny tinkering by comparison.

A HARMLESS PLEONASM?

When reproached that the mighty slogan *social market economy* was a meaningless string of words, Chancellor Erhard calmed his critics by agreeing that it was a pleonasm, but a harmless one. His "but" signified that harmlessness excused the sin of passing off mumbo-jumbo as if it had any identifiable sense.

Can a misuse of language in grave and great matters of state and society be really harmless? The pleonasm *Social Justice* inspires doubt.

In the preceding section, I have set out what seems to me a not implausible argument that poverty is prolonged by significant fiscal measures against inequality and that the poor are not getting a very good bargain when income is redistributed in their favor. However, such a calculation fails to reckon with egalitarian passions and the strong need egalitarians feel to show the moral superiority of their stand. If equality is a moral imperative, never mind the hypothetical Dollars and Cents that some gain or lose.

Justice is self-evidently superior to injustice, and supporting argument would simply be silly. If this is true of justice and injustice, it is surely also true of *Social Justice* and *social injustice*? Most people just nod this through, just as they nod through that growth is good but the inequality linked to it offsets some of the goodness. In both cases, the misuse of words passes unnoticed and minds are schooled to think largely in terms of a fake vocabulary.

Justice has a definite meaning that resists the indeterminacy that sentiments and passions would bring to it. Its definite meaning resides in the rules that just acts respect and unjust acts violate.

If *Social Justice* means anything, it simply means justice. If so, we know its rules; *social injustice,* like any other, is a violation of the set of rules that define all justice. It is, after all, but a pleonasm.

However, all pleonasms are not recognized as such in the lazy, nonrigorous mind. A vacuum is felt: *Social Justice* must surely involve something different from common and garden justice. For this to sound and feel plausible, some rule or rule system must be imputed to it that is separate from the rules of justice and may even contradict it—as, regarding the rules of property and contract, it must do.

The vacuum inside the empty word-shell *Social Justice* is filled with the rule of equality and richly proliferating particular applications of that rule, ranging from "positive rights" and progressive taxation to nonselective admission to schools and universities, anonymous applications for jobs, and a host of other ingenious egalitarian regulations, many of them expensive and counterproductive and some verging on the absurd and comic.

However, with equality identified as the defining content of *Social Justice,* it rises to the rank of a moral imperative in the same self-evident manner as justice itself. It neither requires argument nor permits it. It is clearly not a "harmless pleonasm" now, if it ever was one. Owing its moral rank to the careless or cunning misuse of language, it has turned out to be one of the major forces that needlessly perpetuate poverty in the world.

4. THE "JUSTICE" THAT OVERRULES THE RULES OF JUSTICE

It is a hackneyed story, but fits the present context too well to resist retelling it: The traveler asks the passing Irishman the way to Enniskillen. The Irishman replies that if he wanted to get to Enniskillen, he would not start from here.

Hartmut Kliemt (1998) rightly reproaches theories of justice that, much like the Irishman in the story, would start from somewhere else, from a tabula rasa, a hundred grains of manna to be divided among us all, a cake to be sliced, an Original Position, or—a concession to reality?—from the purported genetic survival strategy of the prehistoric hunter-gatherer that is to be understood as the precursor of the Original Position. Since he knows that we can only start from where we are, Kliemt denies himself the pleasure of showing up the inconsistencies and self-contradictions of the several theories of justice that have been launched to occupy the terrain vacated by the retreat of utilitarian ethics. He brushes them aside as irrelevant to reality; hence he treats as irrelevant, too, whether they are well-constructed or jerry-built. He makes an exception, though, of contractarian theory, which he condemns explicitly for postulating a hypothetical contract concluded in hypothetical circumstances by hypothetical people. The condemnation seems to me richly deserved. However, his main interest is not in asking what would be just. He wants to start from the status quo shaped by what in Western democracies passes for the rule of law and its confrontation (or accommodation) with the de facto claims of what he, true to his magnanimously conciliatory nature, agrees to call "distributive justice."

The present writer, who is much less good-natured, would line up

From *RMM* (*Rationality, Markets and Morals: Studies at the Intersection of Philosophy and Economics*), ed. Max Albert, Hartmut Kliemt, and Bernd Lahno, 0 (2009): 267–71. *http://www.rmm-journal.de/*. Reprinted by permission.

the combatants differently and in particular would deny them the advantage of calling themselves by misleading names. For if we bear in mind that the status quo is itself a distribution of goods and bads, benefits and burdens, rights and obligations, acquittals and sentences (or a macro-distribution of these things made up of micro-distributions of them), it must have reached this distribution by the operation of the rules of property and contract and the exercise of liberties. If it so happens that some part of the distribution has resulted from a breach of the rules or the violation of liberties, redress is due according to the same rules. All distribution is a self-contained and self-correcting result of fully enforced rules that delineate just and unjust, optional and obligatory. Whether all parts and aspects of a distribution are seamlessly encompassed by the rules is an open question that arises in regard to discretionary rewards or charges, and is not of paramount importance. The converse of the question, though, is not open. All distributions may not be matters of justice, but all justice is distributive. To speak of "distributive justice" is a strict pleonasm like wet water or female woman. To reserve the name of breaches of justice that replace a rule-based distribution by something different, i.e., a redistribution, is fraudulent usurpation of the word "justice." The fraudulent effect subsists even if the misuse of the word was not due to deliberate deceit.

Trying to limit the damage, in the remainder of this paper I will avoid the term "distributive justice," for the adjective "distributive," redundant as it may be, designates any and all justice and does too much honor to what is, in my view, a systematic breach of the rules of justice. Failing a cleverer and less compromising alternative, I will henceforth call it "social justice."

Damage is still liable to be done, for it is confusing to use the word "justice" to denote a practice that, I shall argue, is in a strict sense unjust. At least, however, the clumsy adjective "social," though meaning precious little, is there to warn us that "social" justice is a different animal from the justice whose rules it overrules.

Kliemt holds that different rules of justice govern distributions in the Aristotelian community and in the Hayekian "Great Society." Perhaps one should add to the community the Enterprise Association of Michael Oakeshott (1996), an idea of society he abhors, that places distributive duties on people they would not have if they were not engaged in a common enterprise. The idea is not implausible, but looks difficult to apply; for what I feel is a community strikes you as an enterprise association, while he thinks that it is really a "great society," and I cannot imagine the sort of evidence that would reveal who of the three of us is right about the type of society we all three inhabit.

James Buchanan once[1] told a parable about a party of fishermen going out in a boat. Some fished from the starboard, the others from the port side. The starboard crew made a rich haul, the port crew caught nothing. They went share-and-share-alike as if each had contributed equally to the catch. Buchanan felt that any other distribution would have been unjust.

But this conclusion does not come as a matter of course. There might have been a local custom of equal shares (with something reserved for the boat), or perhaps an understanding that on this trip equal shares will be the rule. Failing custom or understanding, however, there is nothing to establish a presumption for equal sharing. If any rule of justice can be applied, it is "finders keepers" with a share set aside for the use of the boat. Whether we are in the community or the "great society" depends on the rule of justice, if any, that governs the case in hand, rather than vice versa. The rules of justice rooted in basic conventions seem to change but little cross-culturally, even if their elaboration in common or statute law differs as between states.

What is, to use fashionable language, "hardwired" in civilized man in any type of reasonably civilized society, great or small, is two sets of rules with a small and uncertain overlapping segment between them. One we might call the justice of property. It takes care of the integrity of persons and their property, the keeping of reciprocal promises, the protection from nuisances and incivilities. It answers most questions of right or wrong, free or unfree. The other set could be called the justice of equality. It settles questions of distribution not automatically determined or deliberately decided by the justice of property. In fact, it would have little relevance, and might not even be recognized as a distinct set of rules, if the justice of property were elaborate enough to settle all questions of distribution. Requiring equality in distributions not otherwise determined springs from acceptance of the axiom

1. Personal communication.

that like cases must be treated alike. Since all cases are both like and unlike each other, likeness reduces to cases being "relevantly" functions of the same variable, other variables being ignored as irrelevant. For example, if the relevant variable for the distributions due to two workmen is the number of hours each has worked, equality demands that the one who worked twice as long as the other should get twice the wages. This is the familiar Aristotelian equality in its simple form. However, a distribution may be composed of many different simple equalities. Take, for example, a micro-distribution such as a firm's payroll. Some employees may be paid according to hours worked, others according to skill, yet others by seniority, while the managers' pay may be governed by responsibility. The payroll displays much inequality, but it is in fact a compound of a number of simple equalities, each the function of its relevant variable. In this micro-distribution, the justice of contract and the justice of equality may overlap: the wage scales may be settled by contract, but if they diverge widely from the justice of equality, they will be a source of disapproval.

Radical egalitarians will disregard compound equalities and condemn a distribution that is in effect a compound equality for failing to be a simple equality. They will attack it like bulls in the china shop, ironing out the apparent inequalities and thus devastating the underlying compound equality which was in perfect compliance with the justice of equality.

Some distributions are entirely discretionary, independent of consent by the recipient. The marking of examination papers, the award of prizes and honors, the sentencing of criminals (within broad limits), or the furloughs of frontline soldiers all fall in this category. Inasmuch as justice can be resorted to in the awarding of such discretionary goods or bads, it is the justice of equality that can be of albeit limited help. The justice of property is, of course, not concerned.

One of the many things that discussions with Hartmut Kliemt have made clear to the present author is that there is no injustice *stricto sensu* unless there was an unjust act to bring it about. Unjust states of affairs are not born by immaculate conception, nor are they auto-generated. Moreover, the unjust act that serves as their necessary condition must not simply be one that most of us would disapprove of. It must be an actual, ascertainable breach of a rule of justice. Obedience to the rules and redress of disobedience make a just state of affairs at least logically possible.

Reflection on the nature of "social" justice and more particularly on what may distinguish it from justice *tout court* and earn it the adjective "social," leads to the conclusion that seems merely formal but, if right, sheds light on political practice of the day. Social justice has no rules. None can be discovered by logical or factual inquiry. Instead of rules, it operates by staking claims to specific changes in any existing distribution. However, as it has no rules, it recognizes no state of affairs as socially just. All its claims can never be fully satisfied and a socially just state of affairs created, because there are infinitely many redistributive claims capable of serving someone's interests and the satisfaction of any number of such claims must still leave any number unsatisfied.

Any person whose claim was satisfied in a redistribution may have further claims under the new distribution.

It is widely believed, I think on no solid ground, that social justice does have a rule, namely the reduction and ultimate abolition of inequalities, and that the social justice and the egalitarian agenda are synonymous. Dealing for the moment only with money incomes this would mean that once all incomes above the mean were cut off at the mean level and redistributed to those having below-mean incomes, equality having been reached, a socially just state of affairs will have been reached. But this is only too obviously not the case. Equal money will leave many inequalities and, worst of all, create new nonmonetary ones. Moreover, monetary equality will generate claims of social justice on grounds of unequal desert, unequal need, merit goods, or some less plausible pretext. Since there is no rule in social justice for ruling out claims on certain grounds, and since substitute grounds could always be found by claimants, any given distribution resulting from redistribution would bear in itself reasons for renewed redistribution. This mechanism is not the same as the "cycling" that characterizes, for instance, a three-person distribution game, though it resembles it to some degree.

In justice, redress can only follow a breach of a rule. In social justice, a claim for a redistribution is not grounded on any rule. It is simply a good try. Whether it is satisfied depends on the politics of the time and place. Where political decisions ultimately depend on majority vote, claims in social justice that ostensibly or really favor the poor have a better chance of being satisfied than claims having no income or class bias, but this will not necessarily be the case. Measures favoring the poor at the expense of everybody else will usually command sympathy, but sympathy does not make them less unjust.

Kliemt is persuaded—as are most social scientists and most intelligent laymen, though the present author is trying to make the contrary case—that enforcement of the rules of justice can only be assured by a central authority with coercive power to raise the wherewithal by taxation. Taxation is almost inevitably redistributive. Hence the legal order presupposes coercive redistribution. The argument can be extended to all public goods if they, too cannot be provided by some mechanism of voluntary cooperation. Willy-nilly facing the danger of slippery-slope arguments, Kliemt regards a "minimal welfare state" as the provider of the legal order as a necessary condition of social coexistence. He is, however, also persuaded that there are good reasons for calling a spade a spade. Instrumental redistribution should not be dressed up as distributive or social justice (Kliemt 1998, 635).

The logical and semantic muddle of assimilating redistribution to justice is indeed hard to pardon and there is not the slightest reason why one should pardon it. But it is even more unforgivable that the sloppy language of "social" justice has by and by become, by force of relentless repetition, a bearer of moral truth. Mild-mannered, courteous, and indulgent as always, Kliemt regards the deceitful exploitation of the persuasive terms "distributive" and "social" justice more in sorrow than in anger. More anger, more contempt, or more of both might have been unseemly, but not undeserved.

REFERENCES

Kliemt, H. (1998). "Distributive Justice," in: P. Newman (ed.), *The New Palgrave Dictionary of Economics and the Law,* Bd. 1, London: Macmillan, 630–35.

Oakeshott, M. (1996). *The Politics of Faith and the Politics of Skepticism,* New Haven–London: Yale University Press.

PART 2

Inadvertent Surrender, Real Politics, and Rational Man

1. THE INADVERTENT SURRENDER
SPREADING THE STATE, SHRINKING LIBERTY

"It is a great law of social development that the movement from slavery to freedom is also a movement from security to insecurity of maintenance."
Arnold Toynbee, *Lectures on the Industrial Revolution in England*

The movement in the motto may go either way, between slavery and freedom, security and insecurity of livelihood; it is open in both directions. It is not the road that decides the way, but the traveler who takes it—which is as it should be, as long as he knows where he is going.

This paper is mostly inspired by a composite of two ideas about travelers and their world. One is the rather trite one that most tangible and intangible things we value have some cost, so that having more of one implies having less of others, where the "less" may mean opportunity as well as actual possession and enjoyment. Trade-offs are more characteristic of earthly existence than mutually enhancing complementarity; we can seldom if ever have it altogether both ways. The second idea is a little less trite. It is that in matters political, the vast majority of people act as if they believe that they can have it altogether both ways.

The reason for this is not only man's ingrained *penchant* for wishful thinking, though that is real enough. A probably more important cause seems to me that in our personal dealings the cost of getting more of one thing by giving up something else is manifest, a matter of visible, easily perceived experience; the same is not the case for political choices. Here, the cost side of a trade-off is not manifest. It seeps through a highly elaborate labyrinth of communicating vessels permeating the entire society and is distributed among its members, often in

The second half of this article first appeared as "The Maximizing State," in *The Independent Review* 15 (2010): 5–18. Reprinted with permission from *The Independent Institute*© 2010, The Independent Institute.The first half of the article is previously unpublished;© 2015 by Liberty Fund, Inc.

occult ways. Its incidence on a given individual is hard to discern. He may quite excusably ignore it. He will in due course discern the cumulative weight of the costs of the multitude of trade-offs he participated in, find it excessive, blame "the system" or "the politicians," and vainly seek remedy in demanding other trade-offs whose cost to himself he will likewise overlook.

This suggestion must seem impressionistic, diffuse, and nonrigorous to a fault. However, I believe it can be formulated more tightly and supported by reasonably disciplined deductive argument. Doing so is the set purpose of this paper. It will attempt to reduce the whole process to a progressive surrender of freedom and to its corollary, a spreading of the state, where the surrender of freedom is in large measure inadvertent, a product of short views and loose habits of thought.

In what follows, I shall use "freedom" and "liberty" interchangeably, as synonyms.

PERFECT FREEDOM

Malformations of the Concept of Freedom

Modern political theory employs a variety of formulations of the concept of liberty. Many of these seem to me ill-conceived and barren for purposes of further argument. Ranged in no particular order, some of these are sketched below.

Necessary Coercion. For Hayek, a state of affairs is free if only necessary coercion is exerted to enforce just conduct and to raise the means needed to provide useful services.[1] (It is perhaps not surprising that unnecessary coercion is not consistent with freedom.) Since the purposes for which coercion is admissible as necessary are open-ended, this concept of freedom is underdetermined. Freedom is defined by the coercion that must protect it, and coercion by the freedom it is needed to protect.

Positive and Negative Liberty. Berlin[2] believed that one could distin-

1. F. A. Hayek, *The Constitution of Liberty* (London and Chicago: University of Chicago Press, 1960), 12, 21; and F. A. Hayek, *New Studies in Philosophy, Economics, and the History of Ideas* (Chicago: University of Chicago Press, 1978), 144.

2. Isaiah Berlin, *Two Concepts of Liberty* (Oxford: Oxford University Press, 1958).

guish not one, but two concepts of liberty. One, the positive, requires that some or all should be able to do X. The other, negative, requires that some or most individuals should not be prevented from, or threatened with sanctions for, doing X. Pursuing peaceful purposes is a positive freedom; pursuing them unobstructed and under no threat or intimidation is a negative one. Freedom of speech is usually held to be a "positive" freedom, but its content differs not at all from the "negative" one of no gagging and no intimidation or sanction against speaking freely. One need hardly labor the obvious point that the two are identical and add nothing to their common meaning. On the other hand, they leave a blank where there should be some enlightenment about what kind of acts may be performed (are "lawful") by whom, or what the relation is between freedom and the authority to impose prohibitions and render some acts unfree.

Acceptability. Some authors (notably Brian Barry)[3] identify liberty with acceptability; a free act is acceptable (though the reverse need not be so). This, of course, cannot be taken literally, for all feasible acts are "acceptable," including the choice of the alternative that is usually cited as the argument-stopping example, the accepting of starvation wages to avoid the next-worse alternative of starving to death. Instead of meaning it literally, these authors must mean "acceptable" in some figurative sense, perhaps as morally justified. Be that as it may, very unpalatable alternatives are classed as unfree. More surprisingly, very attractive alternatives are also said to be unfree, because they have compelling force and are "impossible to refuse." We seem then to be left with a narrow zone of free alternatives that are no more and no less than acceptable. (Such reasoning must deny that "preferred choice" can be free, for the preference predestines it to be chosen, or indeed that it is anything but an oxymoron, for "preferred" *means* chosen. Only indifference would be innocent of such vices, but then some doubt that "indifference" can possibly be a descriptive term.)

Mutual Compatibility. John Rawls's[4] first principle of justice revolves around liberty, though it is difficult to divine the precise concept he has in mind. He restricts it by prohibiting any trade-off of any part of

3. Brian Barry, *Justice as Impartiality* (Oxford: Oxford University Press, 1995).
4. John Rawls, *A Theory of Justice* (Oxford: Clarendon Press, 1972).

liberty at whatever rate against anything else except a greater liberty—a restriction which people would not normally accept or respect. In some other respects, however, he seems to leave liberty completely without restrictions or frontiers by treating it as a *maximand* subject only to the compatibility of everyone's maximum with the maxima of everyone else. Moreover, this condition applies to "basic" liberties and does not mention nonbasic ones, the latter presumably meaning the entire residual. If that is the case, are we to take it that since my stealing your purse is compatible with your stealing my purse, we both have the freedom to do it? Finally, grasping his principle is made even more precarious by his referring not to liberty, but to a "right to liberty," a curious formulation, since unless the right in question is really a privilege only some have, or the object in a contract only some have agreed on with others, it is possessed equally by everybody and is vacuous: all must have the same "right to liberty" and all must have the same "liberty" convey the same message. If this critique sounds too harsh, let us look at the chapter and verse: "Each person is to have an equal right to the most extensive total system of equal basic liberties compatible with a similar system of liberty for all."

Capability. Amartya Sen[5] wishes to enlarge the ordinary-language concept of freedom, adding to it institutions, facilities, and endowments that either widen the feasible set from which acts can be selected and performed, or facilitate the performance, or both. Thus, wealth, income and credit, law and order, active and properly regulated markets, an adequate physical infrastructure, education, information are, implicitly or explicitly, all incorporated as constituent parts of freedom. What they jointly amount to, of course, is a nice, properly functioning society that has all it needs to flourish and facilitate the flourishing of all its members, including the poor. Cataloging all the attributes of the social state of affairs that are conducive to development has no doubt some merit. However, their identification with freedom has not. Most, if not all, of the attributes that make for "capability" to act are independent concepts in their own right. It is to the advantage of analysis to be able to account for each or any of them separately; submerging them in an enlarged megaconcept seems to me a loss of clarity and a handicap to analysis.

5. Amartya Sen, *Development as Freedom* (New York: Anchor, 2000).

De Facto Liberty: The Ring Fence

The freedom concepts touched upon in 1.1 are all partly or wholly normative, stating what ought to be the case for it to be worthy to be regarded as free. There is nothing erroneous about this, though one may doubt whether this is the right starting point for further thought about what ails freedom or what its future might be. For as we well know, "ought" is logically dependent on "can," and "is" a focal member of the class of "can"; it might be a good idea to take it for a starting point.

Every individual at any time is faced with a set of feasible acts from which he can choose to perform some at the cost of forgoing others. If he is Robinson Crusoe on the desert island before becoming aware of the man Friday, his choices are all free. As far as he can tell, performing a feasible act entails no risk of sanction on the part of another person, though it may be sanctioned by Nature or his own sense of moral fitness and dignity. When he shares with other persons the territorial or social sphere over which his feasible set extends, he must also consider the risk of sanctions on their part if his act is liable to damage their interests or offend their sentiments. We may conveniently grade all acts contained in his feasible set according to the probability-weighted cost to the actor of incurring the relevant sanctions. We may order them so that acts carrying little or no risk move toward the center and those entailing high risk of grave sanction move toward the edge of the set. Near the edge, feasible acts will be described as unfree, near the center as free, with a somewhat fuzzy frontier zone separating the rather free from the rather unfree.

However, instead of a spectrum or continuum, we may find a clear and sharp rule system that neatly separates the feasible set in two, the free and the unfree, the "may" or the "must not," a binary alternative in which the rule-based sanctions are either prohibitive or absent, a convenient simplification one may employ while bearing in mind that reality is less neat and at best approximates the clear dividing line. I shall call the latter the "ring fence" that encloses the free subset of the feasible set. Within the ring fence, there is de facto freedom.

I submit that the origin, nature, and position of the ring fence should be held at the center of our interest when considering liberty both in the descriptive and in the normative mode. It is perhaps needless to insist that in the descriptive mode, the ring fence may be a sort of shameful Berlin wall, leaving a de facto freedom that with but little poetic licence one would call servitude. It could also enclose an area which most observers would describe as reasonably free.

Defining liberty as that part of a person's, or society's (as the case may be), feasible set delimited by a ring fence of rules that exclude from it the feasible acts that must not be performed, implies that we treat the feasible set as given. An increase in a person's or group's wealth or knowledge does not enlarge the feasible set and its free subset under consideration; it creates a new feasible set to be considered separately. The reason for this manner of proceeding has been set out in 1.1 in the context of Amartya Sen's idea of an enlarged freedom concept in which riches and facilities get assimilated into freedom.

Collective Choice

All individual choice is unanimous, for even if made despite doubts and contradictory preferences, the choice signifies that the chooser has not disagreed with himself. Collective choice is usually nonunanimous. By collective choice, one or some persons choose a state of affairs for themselves and others, where the latter may not agree with the choice but cannot avoid accepting it. The chosen state of affairs may be uniform, entailing the same outcome for all; for instance, in the chosen situation all must observe a curfew at 9 p.m. However, more interestingly, the chosen state may entail a better outcome for the choosers than for those they have chosen for; e.g., the latter must observe the curfew while the former go out in search of entertainment.

Dictatorship, where one chooses for all, including oneself, is a special case of collective choice.

Why do those who do not agree with the choice made for them obey it nonetheless? In what could be characterized as ad hoc cases, they obey because they recognize the superior power of those imposing the choice, so that resistance would be more costly than the probability-weighted result of resisting successfully. Obviously, the lesser that probability, the smoother will be the application of collective choice. A strong war band holding an unarmed town to ransom illustrates this case.

As opposed to the ad hoc situation, the systematic imposition of collective choice does not rely on raw power alone. When a type of choice situation is recurrent, acquiescence in it becomes to some extent habitual and requires little show of raw power, especially if resistance in the past has been harshly punished. The tendency to habitual acquiescence even when faced with only symbolic armed power is vastly enhanced when the collective choice in question is encased in a formal rule, and doubly so if the rule gains legitimacy either by the sheer passage of time or by its conformity to some solemn event (a coronation) or quasi-contract proclaimed to be ground-laying (a constitution). Closely related to such legitimizing devices is the widely held presumption in favor of predictable rule-based decisions even if many particular decisions made in conformity with the rule are unfavorable if not downright odious. The propensity to approve of systematic conformity to rules will be the greater the further removed is the collective choice from the limiting case of dictatorship and the nearer it moves in the direction of decisions by simple head count with bare majorities being decisive. Thus, democracy is quite regularly praised as the ideal political regime even by those who are systematically on the losing side of the decisions it typically generates, notably in the field of taxation.

Moving from the ad hoc and arbitrary to the rule-based types of collective choice is highly likely pari passu to reduce the cost of imposing these choices. It liberates some of the power which would otherwise have to be employed to enforce them. Plainly, however, the greater willingness of those for whom choices are made, to submit to them because they are made in a particular mode, is a sign of what we might diagnose as inadvertent surrender (cf. section 3).

Surrender of the case-by-case weighing of the costs and benefits that belong to the obey-disobey alternative in favor of a generalized acceptance of the rule system and habitual obedience to each of its rules effectively becomes a rule in its own right. I propose to call it the "rule of submission," a name which I believe to be more suggestive of its function and its importance than the innocuous term "rule of recognition" which Hart uses in *The Concept of Law*.[6]

The Ring Fence of "Perfect Freedom"

Real-life ring fences enclosing the area of freedom and separating free from unfree acts within a person's or a whole society's feasible set are

6. H. L. A. Hart, *The Concept of Law* (Oxford: Oxford University Press, 1961).

made of collective choices enforced by power wielded by the decision maker assisted, under rule-based choice processes, by the "rule of submission." There is a prima facie objection of principle to such ring fences: they are imposed by some on others even if the others passively submit to them and do not consider the alternative.

Is a ring fence conceivable that does not bear this taint?

"Conceivable," of course, need not mean that it is likely to occur in real life. For plausible reasons, it is improbable to occur and is improbable to survive for long if it does occur. That, however, does not deprive the question of importance. "Perfect freedom" is, or at least should be, treated as a concept whose role as a standard of reference in political philosophy is as important as is that of "perfect competition" in economics, though we are no more likely to come across the latter than the former.

One of the most valuable contributions of game theory to political thought is the insight that rational individuals motivated by what is ordinarily called self-interest will, without having to consult or bargain with one another, adhere to coordinated behavior patterns that assure them mutual benefit. The benefit or "payoff" may not be at its potential maximum. It need not be Pareto-efficient itself but will in any case be a Pareto-improvement upon the uncoordinated alternatives. In the corresponding equilibrium no single individual has a reason to deviate from equilibrium play, nor has anyone a reason to wish that another single individual will deviate. Adopting the coordinated behavior is spontaneous. It is called a convention. Conventions function as rules that persons must follow on pain of losing some of their "payoff" either because the convention is self-enforcing by its nature (e.g., driving on the same side of the road) or because its observance is enforced by another convention (e.g., the rule that decent bystanders help catch the thief).

J. S. Mill held that while people's own good is not a legitimate reason for using power to impose some behavior upon them, harm to other people is such a reason. His "harm principle" has ever since served as justification for a seemingly endless flow of collective choices. This should cause no surprise, for "harm" is an open-ended category, defying definition that would limit its reach. All manner of acts can be construed as being harmful to somebody. This becomes not only figuratively but also strictly and literally the case once omissions come to be as readily branded "harmful" as commissions. The tendency to do so underlies much egalitarian and welfare advocacy. It was put quite explicitly by Joseph Raz,[7] who stated that not helping someone is to harm him.

While the "harm principle" is best consigned to oblivion, harm as a cause of painful physical or mental sensations is real enough and seems to be at the origin of social conventions. Manifestly, there are harms that are common enough, significant enough, and above all manageable enough by everyone adopting a certain behavior to provide sufficient cause for a convention to cope with that particular harm to emerge by spontaneous coordination. In other words, the spontaneous emergence of conventions acts as a selection mechanism that scans the inchoate magma of harms and chooses some to be dealt with by the adoption of suitable coordinated behavior.

I submit that it is by this spontaneous selection process that certain harms come to be regarded as having *moral status,* together constituting most if not all of morality. They are ethically prior to *rights.* The independent moral status of the latter is questionable, and so is their role in regulating social behavior except in the context of contracts.

The Redundancy of "Rights," and Why It Matters

Though it is perhaps a digression, it seems advisable to enlarge upon rights and their putative role in defining liberty. Since the well-deserved decline of classical utilitarianism, it has become the custom in political philosophy to speak of "rights-based" order,[8] but it remains unclear where rights come from, why we suppose that they exist and command respect. Little if any reliance is placed on such potential origins of rights as divine revelation or natural law. Instead, their existence is treated as self-evident. Nozick, in the opening sentence of his *Anarchy, State and Utopia,* feels safe simply to declare that "Individuals have rights"[9] without furnishing reasons why we should believe this.

7. J. Raz, *The Morality of Freedom* (Oxford: Oxford University Press, 1986), 416–17.

8. J. L. Mackie, "Can There Be a Right-Based Moral Theory?" *Midwest Studies in Philosophy* 3, no. 1 (September 1978): 350–59, discusses the conceptual side of basing a moral theory on "rights."

9. Robert Nozick, *Anarchy, State, and Utopia* (New York: Basic, 1974), ix.

Rights *stricto sensu* are options enabling the holder to require the execution of an act (or the forbearance from one) by another person who is under a matching obligation to do so. Thus, they can be created by reciprocal promises (contracts). The latter manifestly exist, are vastly important, but they are also ad hoc and do not regulate behavior beyond the object of the contract itself. "Rights" in the sense used by much modern political thought, on the other hand, are universal regulators in that they are the ramparts of liberty; it is because rights must not be violated that liberty must be respected, and it is the completeness of the system of rights that makes for complete liberty.

If, as I claim, the existence of such rights is devoid of evidence and rests on a gratuitous assertion, there is no reason why liberty should not be violated. Nor is it coherent to argue that such a thing as liberty exists at all. Consider, however, that in order to "violate a right," an act has to be committed that in terms of the immediately preceding analysis has the status of a wrong. "People's rights must not be violated" becomes meaningful if it is explicated as "people have the right that no wrong should be done to them" or more simply "people have the right not to be wronged." This is nonsensical, and the word "right" turns out to be redundant. If the act in question is wrong, there is nothing further to be said; the rules take care of it and if they do not, nothing else will. If, on the other hand, the act is not wrong, no right can make it so, and it cannot be a violation of liberty. (The reader will have perceived that in the spirit of this analysis, a law imposed by collective choice that forbids an act that under purely conventional rules would be free, is a violation of liberty and a wrong.)

It may bear repeating in the present context that there is a strict meaning of the word "rights" that admits no confusion: it is the option of a party P to require the performance of (or forbearance from) an act Q from another party R where R is under an obligation to perform or yield up Q if P exercises his option by telling him to do so. "Right" and "obligation" are the two members of an indissoluble pair.

As was seen above, "right" or "rights" may be employed with other intended meanings that transpire from the text. Characteristically, they refer to P and Q while omitting R; a person P is said to have a right to have or do Q and it is left unsaid who will yield or furnish Q to him. On a closer look, it turns out that the putative right does not exist except as a normative assertion, and is redundant. There is an apparent exception to this conclusion. It is when "right" is used as a power or entitlement some have and others similarly placed do not (e.g., a courtier has the "right" to sit down in the king's presence, but others do not). But here "right" is misused and means "privilege." All this, the reader might complain, is of interest only to the purist and maybe not even to him. However, it would be hasty to think so, for the matter has much political significance, concealed as it may be by our own inadvertence.

For what difference does it make whether we say "We have a right to do Q" or "We are at liberty to do Q"? (The composite "We have a right to the liberty of doing Q" must signify that only we have this liberty and others do not, a case we have discussed in 1.1. in relation to Rawls's formulation of his First Principle that we now may safely ignore.)

Both expressions mean the same in practice; in terms of a feasible set that contains all our acts, both free and unfree divided from each other by a "ring fence," both expressions say that Q is inside the ring fence, it is free, and we incur no risk of sanction if we perform it. "We are at liberty to . . ." describes this state of affairs. "We have a right to . . ." adds to it the suggestion it is not the intrinsic quality of Q that saves it from being placed outside the ring fence and leaves it free, but it is a permission that for some unknown reason relates us to it and renders it free; without the permission it would not or at least might not be free. In the former case, everything is free unless it is rendered unfree by the rules that make up the ring fence. In the latter case, everything is unfree unless it is liberated for us by a specific permission or right; acts to which no such right attaches are unfree and hence fall outside the ring fence.

If, as a matter of empirical fact, there exists a ring fence made up of rules, then it is the rules that say whether an act is free, and giving us a "right" to them is redundant. (If the "right" is not redundant, then the rules are.) But the redundancy is hardly harmless, a menial sin of sloppy language. For using "a right" instead of "is free" to do Q implants in the mind the idea that one is free to do Q because one has been endowed with a right to it, and not because the rules do not say that one must not do Q. Except if every feasible act is prohibited, which would be absurd, the "must not" category leaves a residual of free acts, the "may" category; it is fatuous to add that one has a "right" to perform them.

From that fatuity, it is but a short step to a Bill of Rights, or the demand for one. Not only do we submit to collective choice when it legislates the rules of what we must not do, we also expect it to hand down an inventory of "rights" laying down what we may do. We surrender to collective choice not only an authority to single out certain acts for special treatment, but implicitly also to treat with discretionary power all other acts not so singled out in this solemn inventory.

What, then, is the destiny of the large universe of acts that are neither explicitly forbidden nor explicitly made the object of a "right"? When only the "must not" category is explicitly defined ("everything is free unless it is prohibited"), the burden of proof that an act is not free lies with the objector to the act. He can show that there is a valid objection to it, while the defender cannot show that the objection is not valid. We call this the presumption of liberty. In the symmetrically opposite case when only the "may" ("rights") category is explicitly defined (everything is forbidden unless it is allowed), the burden of proof lies with the proponent of the act. He can show that there is a valid reason for allowing the act, while the objector cannot show that there is none. We might call this the presumption of unfreedom. However, in the logical muddle of the hybrid "rights-based" system where there are both rules that prohibit and "rights" that allow, there is no clear presumption either way; it has been tacitly surrendered to the discretion of collective choice that may adjudicate cases according to some conception of the public interest or ideological sympathy.

The Enforcement of "Perfect Freedom"

It will be recalled that in the present scheme of things "perfect freedom" denotes a state of affairs where all choice is either individual or unanimous, collective choice being excluded by design. All rules are "conventions," the result of spontaneous coordination of behavior by individuals motivated by payoff-enhancement. It is a commonly recognized fact of life that a wide range of coordinated behaviors are payoff-enhancing. The emergence of conventions is thus a strong conjecture. If we do not kill peaceful strangers, traders can go and trade in strange places. If reciprocal promises are not breached, contracts with nonsimultaneous execution become possible. If possession generates the presumption of title, the institution of property is established. Life is less unpleasant if people show courtesy to each other than if they do not.

The wonder of wonders that should impress us far more than it does is that this conjecture actually works. Our social infrastructure is a thick tissue of conventions acting as "must not" rules. The most important ones go back to prehistory. The whole tissue is fairly stable over time and shows relatively little cross-cultural diversity.

The essential and most generally occurring conventional rules fall, by and large, into three classes. Rules against torts protect from killing, maiming, and other violent interference with the peaceful pursuits of others; trespass, theft, robbery, and willful damage; usurpation, fraud, and the breach of reciprocal promises. A less well-defined, less stringent, and in part still-evolving class of rules protects against nuisances that may range from unneighborly conduct, rowdyism, and ostentatious flaunting of offensive "lifestyles" to major negative externalities such as water or air pollution. Finally, rules against incivilities are in a cross-culturally less stable class whose name is self-explanatory.

A convention is an equilibrium, though not necessarily a stable one. If coordination between the parties unravels, perhaps because one party attempts to improve his payoff at the expense of the other, a different convention may finally emerge; instead of "do not kill peaceful strangers," it may be "kill defenseless strangers" under which all go about warily and armed to the teeth, and all earn a low payoff (except possibly a lucky few).

However, the survival of beneficial, payoff-enhancing conventions from prehistory or early history strongly suggests that the more favorable of alternative conventions will prevail. They may unravel locally and occasionally, but by and large they subsist. This seems very odd, for many of the most important conventions are prima facie not self-enforcing.

A self-enforcing convention has a simple payoff structure that offers no gain to a player who would deviate from the coordinated strategy. If the rule of the road is to drive on the right, he who suddenly changes to the opposite lane and drives on the left is about to earn a very low payoff indeed. Deviation from the coordinated conduct, however, can be very attractive when the payoff structure does not simply make it self-enforcing. Where residents all trust the conventions that protect property and do not even lock their entrance doors, a robber can greatly improve his payoff by deviating from the common strategy. It is plainly the case that many of the "heavyweight" conventions, having to do with questions of distribution of goods, involve some conflict as well as some benefit, and make deviation tempting for the first mover who earns extra payoff before the other players as second movers adjust their strategy to his (and install locks and alarms).

Prima facie non-self-enforcing conventions, however, can in real life act as if they are self-enforcing and behave as equilibria. The evidence of their longevity suggests that this must be so. One of two possible hypotheses would explain why this may be the case.

Consider first a two-person game in which each player has the option of adopting a strategy that, if met with a coordinated response by the other player, yields the mutually beneficial interaction. However, either player can earn a higher "free-rider" payoff by deviating from the mutually beneficial strategy if the other, behaving as a "sucker," sticks to it. The hypothesis is that at least in some sufficient proportion (and perhaps all) of recurrent games, a deviant strategy by one player provokes the other player to adopt a contingent strategy that punishes the deviation. If a sufficient proportion of players react to deviation by the others by applying the contingent strategy, the probability-adjusted value of the sanction may swamp the excess payoff to be earned by deviation. The net free-rider payoff, adjusted for the sanction, will then fall short of the payoff to be earned by the mutually beneficial strategy. Despite the element of distributional conflict in the game, the temptation to deviate is neutralized and the game will function as a self-enforcing convention. It may be regarded as two conventions combined: the main one, apparent on the surface, in which all or nearly all players always play the coordinated strategy and ignore the temptation to deviate, and a satellite convention that breaks out from under the surface when deviation takes place, and sanctions it. The two jointly are self-enforcing. It should be remarked that a player may well choose to adhere to a satellite convention that involves meting out punishment not only to those others who breach a conventional rule and wrong him, but also to those within his purview who wrong others; for the satellite convention will function more effectively if it demands retaliation not only against wrongs done to the player himself, but against breaches of the rule(s) that do wrongs to other players, as it were, within sight and within earshot. Reciprocity not only helps share the cost of meting out punishment, but also increases the probability of the rule breaker being in fact punished. It may be remarked that if the satellite convention operates with reciprocity, enforcement takes on some of the character of a network and does not depend on any particular interaction being recurrent, for even one-shot games (a person murdered, or swindled out of his life's savings, will cause the contingent punitive strategy of others to "kick in").

There is another hypothesis that would also suffice to explain why apparently non-self-enforcing conventions in fact do enforce themselves. It is widely believed, not without some verisimilitude, that most people are not straightforward payoff-maximizers, but are biased by self-esteem, a sense of decency, fairness, altruism, and a respect for rules per se. Tautologically, these moral sentiments (to give them a name) may be incorporated into "utility payoffs," so that a strategy yielding a payoff of 1 with self-esteem will be chosen rather than one "not rational" or at least that "they do not maximize." Rationality and maximisation would, at all events, be handled with care, a warning whose purport we cannot pursue here.

With all other things equal, this hypothesis about the benign influence of "morally biased" payoffs leading to self-enforcing conventional rules will be the stronger the longer and more fully the rules have been respected. Why this is likely to be so is plain enough and I shall not labor the point.

However, the opposite case, when the rule system has been seriously disrupted with impunity, is worth a moment's thought. A meadow, regularly grazed or cut for hay, grows thick grass and almost no weeds. Once ploughed up, it becomes a forest of weeds unless quickly sown with a cover crop and weeded, sprayed, or both with some intensity. This may be a pointer to why the Somalias and Afghanistans of this world have for so long failed to generate social convention upon which some semblance of order could rest.

To sum up, "perfect freedom" is enforced when the conventional rules that divide the universe of feasible acts into "mays" and "must nots," freedoms and unfreedoms, are themselves self-enforcing equilibria. This will be the case if the punishment that sanctions deviation from the rules, weighted by its probability, reduces the gain from rule breaking to below the gain from mutually beneficial coordinated rule keeping. Administering punishment both to deter harm to oneself and to uphold and protect the rules could itself become a convention in its own right, adhered to by some, not necessarily by all, members of social groups, and may be seen as a satellite of the primary conventions. Moral sentiments and the force of habitual respect for the rules may induce significant proportions of such groups to behave *as if* conventions were self-enforcing and thus make them more reliably self-enforcing than they would be if the deterrent effect of sanctions was alone at work.

THE MAXIMIZING STATE

History seems to demonstrate that a society of perfect freedom, immune from the habit of collective choice, perdures only for small and very poor societies of simple design in relative geographical remoteness that isolates them from other societies. Other than in such increasingly rare conditions, perfect freedom survives only in shreds and fragments in states in which ad hoc or rule-following collective choice predominates. It would be rash to conclude that this transformation is a necessary consequence of some omnipresent cause, an incontrovertible corollary of the human condition, or the nature of any social organization. It would be better theory to propose more modestly with Hume that the transformation is a matter of "constant conjunction" that has always occurred but may or may not occur again in the future.

We need not decide whether collective choice comes to prevail because ordered anarchy is an intrinsically weak structure or because the state is an inherently strong one. A case can be made for either view. In this article, I lay out the factors that always have made, and presumably always will make, the transformation from ordered anarchy to state highly probable.

The State as Unitary Actor

My 1985 book *The State*[10] has been fairly widely criticized on the ground that it is an unwarranted anthropomorphism to treat the state as a unitary actor making decisions the way a person does, selecting them in its calculating mind with reference to its preferences and the conditions that it encounters or expects to prevail. The critics have pointed out reasonably enough that the state is a very complicated and opaque set of bodies and persons loosely connected by some common interests but also separated by conflicting ones, bound by some common rules but also following particular ones of their own and pursuing objectives that pull them in various directions at once. The critique was deserved in the sense that I should have anticipated and met it explicitly rather than taken for granted that readers will see the advantage of imagining the state as a unitary actor about whose decisions certain predictions can be made, instead of treating it more realistically as a chaotic and largely unpredictable witches' cauldron that at best can be described but that defies theory.

An analogy from economics may not disarm the critique but may explain why I believe that it ought to be firmly resisted.

A firm, especially a corporation of a certain size, is a hierarchical organization that functions, as does the state, by command and obedience. Final command rests with the owners and cascades downward by delegation; disobedience of varying degrees is sanctioned by punishments of varying gravity. Within this top-down assembly, a number of subassemblies have some autonomy without which they can function only poorly or not at all. Thus, production, purchasing, design, maintenance, marketing, personnel, and finance, to mention only the principal ones, have a certain latitude to make their own decisions; defend and expand their "turf" and "pull the blanket over themselves"; secure easy objectives, higher capital budgets, greater influence, and more consideration for their activity at top management level; and so forth. In the limit, each of these "subassemblies" may be pulling the firm in a different direction. It would be hard to make a case that the firm is more like a unitary actor than the state.

10. Anthony de Jasay, *The State* (Oxford: Blackwell, 1985; Indianapolis: Liberty Fund, 1998).

Nevertheless, despite sporadic attempts to deal with the firm purely descriptively or a little more ambitiously, imputing to it some behavioral regularity ("firms add a normal margin to cost and sell what they can at that price")—attempts that have borne little fruit—economics has by and large adhered to the theory of the firm that treats it as a unitary actor and imputes to it a single *maximand,* profit, that is the only *point* of having a firm at all, any other objective ("market share," "longevity," or "monopoly power") being potentially rational only if it is at least consistent with profit maximization. This theory of the firm, in increasingly sophisticated guises, has done great service both in promoting rigorous thinking and in helping us to understand reality, and economics would be poorer if it were discarded on the ground that no real-life firm is in fact a unitary actor and that none can ever be "proven" to maximize profit. (Proof is the more awkward to find because the rational *maximand* is the present value of all expected future profits, expectations of the future are not uniform in their level and time pattern, and management may well be more sanguine than the marginal shareholder—hence, the alleged conflict between short and long term.)

I contend that just as no particular firm can be proven to maximize profit, but the behavior of firms in general can be best predicted by assuming that they strive to do so, so the behavior of states can be best understood and predicted by imputing to them a single *maximand.* Sporadically in history and political theory, potential candidates for the role of *maximand* have cropped up. Territory, power, tax revenue, and dynastic security of tenure have been mentioned, although not systematically developed. I maintain that the *point* of sovereign command, of *being the state* at all, is to have power one can use at one's discretion.[11]

The distinction between power *tout court* and discretionary power is crucial. All other things being equal, power reduces to the capacity to have at least some of one's commands obeyed by a relevant population (or, probabilistically, by some portion of it). However, some commands may merely serve to bring about the very obedience that they demand. The state may order its subjects to pay taxes for the maintenance of

11. Geoffrey Brennan and James Buchanan [1980] (1999) frame the state as a unitary actor maximizing taxes, rather than discretionary power.

judiciary and police apparatus designed to intimidate the population into obeying the order to pay these taxes. Alternatively, the state may order people to shore up a dam to protect their own village from being flooded. Obeying this command is in the villagers' own interest. Had the command been instead to join a mass demonstration for world peace and human rights, they might not have obeyed unless the state had driven them or was able to rely on their abundant loyalty. Having one's command of the latter sort obeyed or collecting more taxes than are needed to secure continuing taxpayer obedience and to ensure that the same tax will be raised the next time around is having discretionary power. Such power enables the state to realize objectives that are not instruments for reproducing power. Promotion of a supreme value, patronage of the arts, and establishment of a firmly based kleptocracy are plausible examples of discretionary objectives, among many others.

The Machinery of Maximization

The state's power is exercised by the government as plenipotentiary agent. We may say that for most purposes the government is the personified state. One difficulty about this usage is that whereas the state is best understood as an abstract entity, the government is both abstract and physically existent, consisting of real persons, some of whom can be more completely identified with the government than others. However, theory must live with this awkwardness of reality as it does with so many other things.

Discretionary power is power not required for its own reproduction or maintenance; power is the property of commands being obeyed; and obedience (to the government) is a function of intimidation and allegiance.

In seeking to maximize its discretionary power, the government schematically must "feed" the two "ingredients," intimidation and allegiance, into a kind of machinery where they mix and move along until they "come out" as obedience; obedience, in turn, procures the wherewithal for the intimidation and allegiance to be fed into the machine.

Several processes may lend themselves to turning intimidation and allegiance into obedience and obedience into intimidation and allegiance. The most obvious and in our time the most widely used is, of course, taxation. Using taxes to acquire resources *both* for maintaining a repressive apparatus that will intimidate people into paying taxes *and* for other purposes leaves some of the latter resources available to be used for buying allegiance. If judiciously targeted, the granting of material privileges to some and the redistribution of the resources of some for the benefit of others will create more allegiance and readier obedience to the government than they will cause alienation among the victims of redistribution.[12]

The use of resources merely to generate the obedience that allows the raising of resources of the same magnitude, leaving nothing over for discretionary purposes, is a break-even exercise, an altogether futile drudgery. Although such a futile result is indeed the probable but unintended outcome of attempts to solicit greater allegiance, "break even" is not the aim of running the machinery of maximization, but rather the eventual self-destruction of the aim. Without the ability to yield power that can be employed at discretion for any purpose short of the absurd, *being a state* is a pointless exercise.

The idea of the minimal state that imposes collective choice over only a severely restricted domain and exercises self-denial by not using power to generate discretionary power seems to upset this conclusion. In fact, the minimal state, if it existed, would be an antistate actor whose rational purpose would be the opposite of that of the state, preempting the place that a state can otherwise take and expand in.

Although obedience may yield discretionary power, it is quite unlikely to do so as if the latter were a linear function of the former, increasing in the same proportion as intimidation and allegiance increase. It is a plausible conjecture that beyond a certain degree of required obedience, diminishing returns set in, and more intimidation, combined with more redistribution or not, not only fails to raise discretionary power, but actually decreases it. Discretionary power is maximized when its (rising) marginal cost is equal to its marginal increment, both measured in resources. Naturally, one cannot find this point by calculation. It can be identified more or less successfully only with the antennae of instinctive statesmanship. Taxation, I suspect, may be foolishly excessive, and dictatorship overdone for its own good. Discretionary power is more likely to be maximized with discretion.

12. For the public-choice background, see Mueller 2003.

Inadvertent Surrender: Social Contract and Conquest

Hardly any other cliché or allegory keeps as strong a grip on the mind of both the political philosopher and the ordinary man as the social contract. The reason seems straightforward: social contract theory flatters us into believing that we have conjured up the state not as a matter of misguided, absent-minded, and inadvertent surrender, but of our own clear-sighted will. There is no call to be either rebellious or rueful about it. People had ample reason for entering into it and for honoring its terms. We need not feel a little foolish or ashamed that we could not fail or honor it if perchance we should like to do so, because the contract has turned out to be irrevocable and permanent, admitting neither breach nor renegotiation.

We are not dealing here with the early form of the contract, the one between God and the monarch under which the latter, in exchange for the power granted to him, binds himself to rule in conformity to his divine mandate. Nor do we mean the quasi-social contract by which the monarch consents to a constitution, and in return his people consent to obey him but retain the material means to disobey (refuse to pay taxes, meet force with force, depose the monarch).

The social contract as tacitly understood in contemporary usage is that of Thomas Hobbes ([1651] 1968), by which the people contract among themselves to create Leviathan, who is not a party to the contract but who has the sword to enforce the "covenant," or that of Jean-Jacques Rousseau, a much less solid construction in which the people conceive of the General Will, agree to submit to it, and have no temptation to disobey because recognition of the General Will tells them that they have no interest to do so (it is better to fell and share the stag than to run off and chase the hare).

It is perhaps needless to spell out that the idea of a whole people's unanimously concluding a contract obliging it to anything at all, let alone to surrender to and obey a superior power, is at best an allegory. To suppose that the people should do so and irrevocably commit all future generations to it, having calculated the expected advantages it will bring, is to impute to the people either a reckless acceptance of a great risk or a failure to see that risk at all.

The state, however, has a more down-to-earth genesis by contractual means in which the parties are unaware that by making what may seem to be innocuous agreements, they are creating the viable embryo of a state. The agreements concern the organization of what Robert Nozick calls "protective agencies" specializing in the enforcement of the conventions that hitherto were being enforced by social sanctions (exclusion of the deviant from the benefits of the convention as well as other punishments administered by the plaintiffs and other parties interested in protecting that convention). Many or most people may have incurred enforcement costs involved in punishing deviants, be it no more than boycotting cheats, watching one's property, mending one's fences, and helping neighbors and peers protect their own and the public order. For some, such activities may actually be a source of satisfaction and self-esteem, but others would resent them as a cost and might well welcome an opportunity to unload the duty of rule enforcement on a specialized agency equipped to discharge it. For many, doing so would feel like taking a free ride because they may not realize that in one way or another they have to bear some of the agency's cost. Others may have the illusion that they can escape these costs altogether or bear a smaller amount of them than the benefit they derive from a third party's enforcement of the rules. On these grounds, the scenario of piecemeal surrender of some of the enforcement function to specialized agencies is as plausible as that of the social contract is implausible. The rest follows not as a matter of inexorable logic, but as a matter of great plausibility, from the "slippery slope" argument. Specialized enforcement agencies merge into a single agency that holds sway over a population delineated by ethnic or geographic features. The agency gradually arms itself and disarms the population, arguments of efficiency in enforcement furnishing an adequate excuse for establishing a monopoly position, which is obviously of paramount importance for an embryonic state. The final stage in this scenario of the birth of the state is a move from the agency's protecting the people's property to its protecting their property from all except itself. In this stage, the agency no longer confines itself to obliging the population to cover its costs of enforcing the rules. Instead, it uses its power to extort from society a volume of resources far greater than mere rule enforcement costs and uses part of the surplus to buy the support of selected segments of society to deter any attempts at resistance by other segments. Henceforward, the mechanism of redistribution is in place and available for maintaining society in a situation of surrender and the state in power, with the ultimate objective of maximizing the state's discretionary power.

Pressed into a nutshell, this account of the state's emergence suggests that the free-rider temptation is the Achilles heel of "perfect freedom." This temptation is not a necessary condition of the state's emergence, but it comes close to being a sufficient condition for it. Another such account, likewise very close to being sufficient though not necessary, is that of the territorial conquest of one ethnic group or otherwise distinct population by another. David Hume ([1777] 1986) states categorically that nearly all past and present governments originated in usurpation and conquest. It is difficult to find in history many states of which this claim is not true. It is certainly true of the most outstanding specimens of statehood. The Trojans subjugated the Latins and made Rome. The Franks conquered Gaul and laid the foundations of France. Scandinavian trader-warriors along the route from the Baltic to the Black Sea took the Slavs into their service and established Kiev and other principalities that in due course formed Russia. The Normans vanquished the Saxons and created a united England. The resulting societies were from the outset neatly divided along ethnic lines into conquerors and conquered, governors and governed, a division that provided an outline for the feudal system of control and almost automatically answered any subsequent question of who would command and who would obey. For centuries, the conquered ethnic group surrendered to the conqueror, until the clear dividing line was gradually washed out, and other divisions took over its founding functions.

Ruling by the Rule

We are in the habit of classifying types of government according to the group in society that exercises political power. Thus, we distinguish theocracy, monarchy, oligarchy, plutocracy, and democracy, to mention only some basic types. Another frequently made classification has only a binary alternative: dictatorship and democracy. However, a more fundamental distinction is between a society in which "the king decrees" and one in which "the king in his council decrees." In the latter alternative, the validity of the king's decision is subject to a formal requirement, an embryo of a rule that constrains rule making.

Self-Imposed Constraints. Kenneth Arrow calls a social (his term for *collective*) choice rule a "constitution," and Thomas Schelling calls a constitution a *vow*. Much past and present misunderstanding in political thought might be dissipated by keeping firmly in mind the word *vow* and with it the state's own role in binding collective choice by rules.

When collective choices are made ad hoc as the occasion demands, the state relies on the sufficiency of its power to get the decision obeyed. It seeks neither to spare certain individuals' preferences nor to allow for all of the likely consequences of overriding them. However, it is perfectly possible that the overriding of individual preferences, though quite feasible, costs more in terms of the power that needs to be used and tied up to deter resistance than it accrues advantages to the state from being carried out rather than some alternative.

The economy in the utilization of power that arises from sparing individual choices on some ad hoc occasion without prejudging the likelihood of overriding them on a future occasion is, however, only one part of the gain the state may expect from "self-denial," and it is independent of such self-denial's taking the form of an explicit, declared "vow," a self-imposed rule to govern collective choice. The latter, removing arbitrariness and imparting a certain limited predictability, should further enhance the economy of power.[13] Moreover, because collective choices to conform to a rule or rules are repetitive, obedience to them is apt to become habitual, and hence resistance tends to become eroded. This catalog of the potential advantages of constrained collective choice applies to the case of the constraint's being unilaterally adopted by the state as a matter of prudential calculation, a case known in history as the absolute monarch's "granting a constitution" to subjects whose role is limited to showing greater willingness to obey in return for diminished arbitrariness. A somewhat different case is that of a constitution as an explicitly negotiated bargain between a monarch and the people, governors and the governed, that should further enhance political obedience, albeit at the cost of a more stringent "vow" on the state's part. Imposing greater restraint would induce a loss from forgone collective choices that is greater than the gain from a further reduction in the use of coercive power. The reverse would,

13. On the enhancement of credit, see Stasavage 2003.

of course, be the case if the state imposed less restraint on its exercise of collective choice. The "secret" (a secret because it is not shared with the governed) is to formulate the rule-making rule under which the state can expect to secure the best trade-off between power saved and desired objectives forgone ("forgone" because they would become "unconstitutional")—the maximizing rule of rule making. The constraints must be incorporated in a master rule, or rule of rule making, that provides for mandating the government (and eventually its recall) and delineates the areas in which collective choice may be exercised and individual choices overridden. Perhaps the most prominent element of any rule of rule making is the specification of the manner in which a rule must be made (for example, by the king's decreeing it in his council or by the majority's voting for it under universal franchise)—what Herbert Hart calls "the rule of recognition" that characterized Venice as a plutocracy and earns most modern Western states the name of "representative democracy."

What is the best rule of rule making for a state? We obviously cannot give a specific answer to this question, any more than we can to a question about a firm's ideal business plan. However, a wholly formal statement of what is best may not be completely useless. By "best," we continue to mean the one most likely to maximize the state's discretionary power. Assuming that greater constitutional constraints yield both diminishing returns in terms of the saving of the power needed to secure obedience and increasing costs in terms of forgone collective choices, discretionary power will rise as long as the saving of power is greater than the opportunity cost of forgoing more and more collective choices. The favorable balance between the two will go on increasing, but at a diminishing rate. Maximum discretionary power will be reached as the power saved by ever-stricter self-imposed constraints no longer exceeds the worth of the lost opportunity of making certain collective choices. Needless to say, this point cannot be found by using calculus, although perhaps clever politicians with "feel" for what "pays" can approximate the formal optimum.

As a practical matter, a constitution that it "pays" to adopt is one that appears to bind the government's hands more than it really does or in ways that matter more to the governed than to the government. For example, a constitution might grant habeas corpus and concessions on other "civil rights" even while maintaining the rule of collective choice over individuals' material resources—the rule of rule making that places no explicit restraint on the taxation of income or wealth. History abounds in real-life constitutional examples of this kind.

Paradoxes of the Rule-Making Rule. In a truly rule-bound system of rules, every rule must be the product of the proper observance of some antecedent rule. Ordinary rules of "must" and "must not" have to be made by following the rule of rule making (including, of course, rule change). *That* rule, however, fails to be rule bound unless it, too, is made by observing a higher-order rule of making rules of rule making, and the latter must be made by following a rule of yet another order higher. A truly rule-bound system is therefore an infinite regress of ever higher orders of rules. This property may or may not be a genuine paradox.[14] In any event, it casts serious doubt on the possibility of legitimate birth of constitutions. Constituent assemblies are organs of collective choice through which collective choice legitimizes itself. This procedure is tantamount to collective choice's vesting in itself the power to override individual choice and laying down the limits or conditions under which such overriding is to be regarded as legitimate. Awareness of this circularity presumably induces many political theorists to embrace the fiction that constitutions are really adopted by unanimity or "practical unanimity," in which case collective choice does not legitimize itself, but individual choice does so.

The other major paradox, apparent or genuine but in any case the source of serious preoccupation, concerns the internal logic or structure of the rule of rule making. Like every rule that regulates behavior and the distribution of benefits and burdens, the rule must provide for both sanctions to punish its breach and the enforcement of these sanctions. Consider the following: "The king has ruled that he (in his council) may decide all things except a certain thing. If he decides that thing, the king must punish the king. If the king fails to punish him, the king must punish the king, and so forth." A quasi-legal construction in which enforcement of sanctions for a breach of the rule rests with the rule breaker himself clearly contains a flaw.

"Separation of powers" reputedly provides a remedy for this rather

14. Related paradoxes are discussed in Suber 1990.

conspicuous flaw. It is a pity that Montesquieu's text that immortalized this idea does not distinguish sharply enough between the separation of three basic *functions* of the state, so that the legislative, executive, and judicial functions are carried out by three distinct institutions motivated by different interests. Moreover, the state's *power* to enforce the decisions taken by these institutions and to protect them, but not also to carry out any of these functions, is in no meaningful sense *separated* into parts to match the separate functions. If it were, civil war would probably be an endemic condition. The separation of functions has done honorable service in the United States, as has most of the rest of the U.S. Constitution.[15] One wonders, however, how such separation would perform in the wildly counterfactual case of the Congress's severely limiting its own authority to impose taxes or the Supreme Court's denying Congress's authority to vote taxes and the executive's entitlement to collect them.

In sum, we must be soberly skeptical of the very logic of a rule of rule making—its ultimate claim to legitimacy and enforceability. In most cases, constitutions seem to "work" principally because they are not tested and are not designed to provoke severe tests or to settle severe conflicts between state and society. Most of their practical effect pertains to the regulation of how governments may obtain power and how their tenure may be terminated. Only in a very idealized sense do they "safeguard liberty"; more precisely, the liberties they safeguard are those that the state is fairly willing to remove from the competence of collective choice because doing so permits a more economical use of power spent on staying in power and is thus conducive to maximizing the residue, discretionary power.

Shrinking Freedom. I find it deeply objectionable to speak, along with John Rawls, of "basic" freedoms, a usage that suggests both that some freedoms are "basic," hence important, and others "nonbasic," hence not very important or perhaps even negligible, and also, more insidiously, to say that someone, perhaps the speaker or perhaps "society" speaking through some authority, is entitled to say which freedoms

15. One might refer here as well to the originally Dutch idea of a compound republic that became so important in theories of federalism in America; see Ostrom [1971] 1987.

are "basic" and which are not. I find it equally objectionable to dismiss the presumption of liberty on the grounds, put forward by Joseph Raz (1986, 8–14), that it fails to discriminate in favor of the more important liberties. Setting up a rank order of liberties, some more basic than others and more deserving of protection under the presumption of liberty, is too close to arrogance to be seemly.

Nevertheless, it is a matter of common perception that some curtailments of freedom have a greater impact on an individual's life and that some have an impact on more individuals than do others. It is therefore not good enough simply to observe that "our freedom is shrinking by the day." We need to spell out which of our freedoms are being shrunk. It might be desirable, in addition, to find an objective measure of the shrinkage.

The prohibition of smoking on public premises is one of the most often cited deprivations of liberty. It seems particularly irritating to smokers (and to a sprinkling of high-principled nonsmokers), perhaps because it is recent and the freedom it suppresses is still fresh in the memory. However, it arguably affects only smokers adversely and even them only when they are on public premises. The excuse offered for the interdiction—that smoking exerts a dangerous negative externality on nonsmokers—may or may not be accepted by smokers as relevant and as justification for the violation of one of their freedoms. But even if it is rejected, the loss of the freedom in question is more significant as a precedent than as an actual deprivation.

The shrinking, by various forms of taxation, of a vast array of freedoms—feasible acts offending against no rule—is best considered in this perspective. The acts in question depend on the use or disposal of material resources—opportunities offered by the possession of wealth and the spending of income—that the state preempts. It is as if the act that depends on the resources subject to preemption had been moved from one side of the fence of rules to the other side, from the "may" to the "must not" category. The upheaval is massive, given that many modern states preempt 50 and even 55 percent of their gross national product and that few preempt anything less than 40 percent, if central and local government spending and compulsory social insurance are added up.

To appreciate the peculiar relationship between the state and property (what current usage persists in calling "property rights," which are derivative forms of property and evoke wrong legal connotations), one must revert to its conventional roots in such behavioral equilibria as "first come first served," "finders keepers," and perhaps also queuing. This trace leads to the Humean conception of first possession, its stability, and its "transference by consent," all antecedent to any sort of state. There is logically a presumption of property—that is, of possession signaling good title in the absence of sufficient reason to challenge it.

States at least implicitly undertake to protect property from everyone except themselves. All but fully socialist ones recognize the inviolability of property as wealth (subject to expropriation under "due process" or "due compensation"). Only a tiny minority of states tax wealth, although most tax inheritance. Somewhat oddly, none recognizes the inviolability of property in the form of income, and, as noted earlier, no rule of rule making so much as mentions constraints on collective choice in the matter of writing tax codes (though a couple make pious references to just taxation). Some apologists of the strange asymmetry between the treatment of wealth and the treatment of income contend that pretax income is not property. No one seeks to find good cause in justice for the numerous other forms of taxation. Consumption, sales, and value-added taxes and excise duties pass without questions of legitimacy and the immense restriction of freedoms they represent.

The tax take is "returned" to society *in natura* as publicly provided goods and services. (There are two exceptions: transfer payments that are returned as cash and the state's discretionary spending permitted by its discretionary power.) Nominal national income is almost unaffected, but real national income falls, perhaps substantially. A basket of goods and services made up of health care, education, pensions, and other entitlements is at best worth its money cost to the recipient if by a fluke he would have chosen the same basket had he been free to do so. In all other cases, though, it is worth less to him than the basket he would have freely chosen. However, although the fact of a decline in real income seems to be a necessary truth subject only to minor qualifications, we cannot put even a rough number on it. In any event, we should perhaps not commingle questions of riches with questions of freedom at given levels of riches.

The shrinkage of freedom due to taxation, however, is clearly massive, and we can put a number on it. In modern states, as noted earlier, between 40 and 55 percent of what is produced by the efforts of individuals under the division of labor is preempted and disposed of by collective choice that is endowed with the power to override individual choices. We may well grant that not all liberties require the use of material resources for their exercise. Some authors on the political left enjoy mocking the liberties that do so, calling them liberties to choose between flavors of ice cream. The metaphor is preposterous. Without setting up a hierarchy of noble, less noble, and ignoble freedoms, we may safely contend that the ones that depend on material resources are immensely important, and if half of all riches is removed from the grasp of individuals, the resulting shrinkage of freedom is immensely important, too.

Another Inadvertent Surrender. For as long as states have existed, their rulers and governments have been buying the support of one part of society—initially a small part—by extorting the purchase price from other parts. At the outset, they would buy the close councilors, courtesans, Praetorian guards, mameluks, bishops, abbots, and other spiritual guides of the people, territorial administrators, and tax collectors. The base on which states relied for support, using redistribution in the widest sense to obtain it, was progressively broadened. In medieval and early-modern Europe, it was not unusual for the state to seek the alliance of an entire class, the better to deter another class from disobedience. Alliances between the king and the towns against the nobility were common. The ally was remunerated by tilting economic policy, such as it was, in the ally's favor and by making classes other than the merchants and artisans bear the main burden of wars.

In buying support with the redistribution of privileges, benefits, and burdens to and from selected groups in society, the state was "using power to stay in power." Using power to raise and move material resources and handing them out as bribes in exchange for support formed a more sophisticated manner of proceeding than deterring disobedience and breach of rules by intimidation. This conduct became an ingrained habit. It has also inadvertently led to the surrender of the state's ultima ratio, its discretionary power.

In part for reasons lodged in the history of political thought and particularly the Enlightenment, early in the nineteenth century egalitarian principles began to make their way into the advanced countries' rules of rule making. Competition between political rivals contributed to an evolution in which the granting or termination of the mandate to govern became the privilege of a gradually broadening part of the governed until it finally settled down at what we now consider its terminal form—namely, simple majority voting in anonymity under universal suffrage.

Under this system, assuming that voters cast their ballots exclusively to promote their own ascertainable material interests (an obvious simplification whose saving virtue is that it is not very conducive to woolly verbiage), a sufficient condition for a person or group to gain or retain the mandate to govern the state is the formation of a decisive coalition more interested in voting for him, her, or it (let it be "it"). A voting coalition cannot be beaten by a rival coalition if the former consists of the majority of all voters and no anonymous member of it can be tempted to desert it and join the rival. (Under anonymity, no bribe can be credibly offered to a voter to join a coalition unless the same bribe is offered to all of its members. If anybody can be the median voter, it is impossible to buy the median voter without offering the same price to all voters in the coalition.)

Recall that the offer made to members of a potential coalition is redistributive—that is, that the winning coalition is to be rewarded out of resources taken from the losing coalition(s). A coalition cannot be beaten if no other coalition can offer more to the average member of a simple majority. This condition will be the case if the winning coalition undertakes to tax the richer half of society (*minus* one person) up to its taxable capacity and distribute the proceeds to the poorer half of society (*plus* one person). Note that a coalition greater than the simple majority can be beaten by one having merely a simple majority because the latter can dispose of the taxable resources of a larger losing minority.

It is obvious that any number of potential coalitions can make the same unbeatable offer, each proposing to reward the same poorer half of society with the resources that can be taken from the same richer half, and each limiting its offer only to the members of a bare majority because any larger majority will have to make do with the spoils taken from a smaller minority.

Therefore, if this situation is recognized by at least two of the rivals partaking in the auction to win the mandate to govern, at least two identical electoral programs will be put forward, and the outcome will depend on some random variable, the toss of a coin. (Some modern electoral contests with convergent programs and very close results do resemble this idealized result.)

CONCLUSION

Conducted on a somewhat abstract level, my analysis suggests that in a condition of perfect liberty where all rules emerge as spontaneous behavioral equilibria, individuals will either abandon this freedom without fully realizing that they are doing so (and entrust power to a rule-enforcing agency) or will be made to do so by foreign conquerors to whom they yield. Either way, they bow to collective choice, surrendering freedom rather inadvertently. They gain a measure of what Arnold Toynbee called "security of maintenance." Only a few would rather undo this bargain and seek liberty in ordered anarchy.

The state, personified in the government, seems no more successful than the individual in consciously pursuing an objective rather than inadvertently allowing outcomes to happen to it. Logically, it would seek to maximize the discretionary power that it could devote to purposes of its own instead of solely to those of its supporters, but it ends up by dissipating all of its discretionary power in political competition of its own making. It inadvertently surrenders the potential its initial endowment of power provides. In the process of becoming a redistributive drudge, it is spreading wider as the sphere of freedoms shrinks. Like the firm in the perfectly competitive industry that makes no profit, the state ultimately achieves only its own survival, and no one is satisfied by this relatively pointless result.

REFERENCES

Barry, B. 1995. *Justice as Impartiality.* Oxford: Oxford University Press.

Berlin, I. 1958. *Two Concepts of Liberty.* Oxford: Oxford University Press.

Brennan, H. G., and J. M. Buchanan. 1999. *The Power to Tax: Analytical Foundations of a Fiscal Constitution.* Indianapolis: Liberty Fund.

De Jasay, Anthony. 1985. *The State.* Oxford: Basil Blackwell; reprint 1998, Indianapolis: Liberty Fund.

Hart, H. L. A. 1961. *The Concept of Law.* Oxford: Oxford University Press.

Hayek, F. A. 1960. *The Constitution of Liberty.* London and Chicago: University of Chicago Press.

Hayek, F. A. 1978. *New Studies in Philosophy, Economics, and the History of Ideas.* Chicago: University of Chicago Press.

Mackie, J. L. 1978. "Can There Be a Right-Based Moral Theory?" in *Midwest Studies in Philosophy 3.*

Mueller, D. C. 2003. *Public Choice III.* Cambridge: Cambridge University Press.

Nozick, R. 1974. *Anarchy, State, and Utopia.* New York: Basic Books.

Ostrom, V. [1971] 1987. *The Political Theory of a Compound Republic: Designing the American Experiment.* 2d ed. Lincoln: University of Nebraska Press.

Rawls, J. 1972. *A Theory of Justice.* Oxford: Clarendon Press.

Raz, Joseph. 1986. *The Morality of Freedom.* Oxford: Oxford University Press.

Sen, A. 2000. *Development as Freedom.* New York: Anchor.

Stasavage, D. 2003. *Public Debt and the Birth of the Democratic State: France and Great Britain, 1688–1789.* Cambridge: Cambridge University Press.

Suber, P. 1990. *The Paradox of Self-Amendment: A Study of Logic, Law, Omnipotence, and Change.* New York: Peter Lang.

2. PRESUMPTION OF LIBERTY

A "presumption of X" signifies that X is taken to be the case without requiring argument or evidence to support it. The burden of its rebuttal is on the challenger of the presumption.

The presumption of liberty signifies that an individual is taken to be free to perform any feasible act without having to show that there is no sufficient reason that he should not perform it. The burden of showing sufficient cause against the act (or against this particular individual performing it) is on the challenger. The latter is characteristically the political authority, or the plaintiff in juridical disputes, but may be anybody with access to public rule-making and administration. Sufficient cause may consist of an applicable role prohibiting the act or in enough probability that the act, if committed, would significantly harm another person or persons.

Conventions, customs, and laws make up the rule system intended to guide social behavior. A rule system that runs in terms of prohibitions is favorable to the presumption of freedom: "everything that is not expressly prohibited is (liable to be) free." A rule system that runs in terms of permissions, such as bills of rights, favors the presumption of unfreedom: "everything that is not expressly authorized is (liable to be) prohibited." However, although the nature of the rule system may favor one presumption or the other, it does not logically establish or exclude either.

It is both widely held and widely contested that the presumption of liberty is the most solid foundation one can find for the edifice of classical liberal or libertarian theses.

One sharp criticism of the foundational role of the presumption of liberty, which dismisses it as "an implausible doctrine," condemns it mainly on the ground that it is undiscriminating and gives the same

Republished by permission of SAGE Publications, from *The Encyclopedia of Libertarianism,* ed. Ronald Hamowy (Thousand Oaks, Calif.: SAGE Publications, 2008), 299–300. Permission conveyed through Copyright Clearance Center, Inc.

weight to vitally important as to trivially unimportant freedoms. Condemning it on this ground is like condemning the umbrella on the ground that it protects indiscriminately from the rain not only the great and the good, but the ordinary plodders as well. There may be a case for ranking liberties in a hierarchical order of greater and lesser, as was done notably by John Rawls and his followers, but it is not a liberal case if only because it must invest someone with the power of deciding which liberty is greater than another.

The other, more weighty, attack against the presumption of liberty holds that it depends on the love of liberty or, more precisely, on the imputation of a value to liberty. This dependence makes the presumption of liberty doubly vulnerable. It may be argued that liberty as such has no value and that those who claim a preference for it really like not liberty, but other values they think it would bring, but that can be obtained more directly and more safely without recourse to the presumption of freedom. It also can be argued, reasonably enough, that, although freedom may be valuable, it is not the sole value we pursue. Many believe, rightly or wrongly, that other values in effect compete with freedom, with more freedom causing less equality or security. Hence, the presumption of freedom, far from being a firm foundation, hinges precariously on the trade-offs that happen to prevail among these competing values.

This line of argument is a mistake. The presumption of freedom in no way depends on the love of freedom. It is a pure product of logic and epistemology. Suppose opinion is divided over whether a certain act is (or should be treated as) free. The actor who wishes to perform it contends that it is free, whereas challengers contend that it is not. Propositions that have descriptive meaning are either verifiable or falsifiable or sometimes both. Take the proposition that the act is not free. There may be indefinitely many potential reasons for believing this notion, having mostly to do with the meanings of rules and with putative harms to various interests. The would-be actor can falsify some of them by showing that they are groundless or of insufficient force. But as he falsifies some, others can always be advanced because such reasons are numberless, and although the actor may falsify any large number, he cannot falsify all. Therefore, the actor cannot bear the burden of proof, and, in logic, it would be nonsensical to place it on him.

The challenger, however, is in an altogether different, we may say asymmetrical, position. Any specific reason against the act in question that he thinks is sufficient can be verified by argument and evidence bearing on that reason. If he fails to verify his first reason, he can find a second and marshal evidence supporting that until he either finally succeeds in his challenge or runs out of verifiable arguments. There is nothing logically nonsensical or epistemologically unfeasible about the task of verifying his proposition that the act should not be free. Consequently, he can carry the burden of proof. Until he succeeds in discharging it, the presumption of liberty prevails, as it were, by default.

The presumptions of innocence and property are twin sisters of the presumption of liberty, in that they spring from the same asymmetry between verification and falsification. "You have committed a crime" and "your title to this property is invalid" are unfalsifiable, but verifiable, statements open to proof, but not to disproof. The presumption of innocence does not depend on the "rights" of the accused nor the presumption of property on the economic case for the owner's security of tenure. Like liberty, they owe their status to the nature of the means the mind possesses for telling true from false.

3. ON RIGHTSISM

Both when it seeks to describe and to prescribe, modern political thought proceeds as if it were exploring and shaping a virtual tabula rasa, unimpeded by the deeply rooted status quo that is inevitably in the way. It is either ignored, or reasons are found for sweeping it aside. Mainstream theories of property, liberty, and their functionally necessary complement, justice, suffer from logical and moral defects as a result.

THREE CHILDREN AND A FLUTE

In his influential *The Idea of Justice,*[1] Amartya Sen tells an allegorical story of three children, Anne, Bob, and Carla, in a dispute about who among them should possess a flute. Sen's object is to show that the argument of each child in favor of getting the flute is of sufficient force, difficult to reject, and admits no tradeoffs, so that no compromises can reconcile the three distinct claims. Each aspires to be the single guiding principle of the ideally just society. With his characteristically mild-mannered persuasiveness, Sen leads us to the conclusion that such a single principle may be impossible to find.

A clever device steers the argument to this conclusion. It is that the flute appears to be *unowned.* This means that one can discuss its being *given* to someone without having to *take it away* from someone else. In this sense, the status quo is empty. No one holds the flute and no one has a status quo to defend. Nor is there an impartial third party judging the case made by the defendant. Theorists of justice find it convenient to employ some such device. They show that the just distribution of manna fallen from heaven is equal sharing. They describe the way the national cake should be sliced without remembering that

From *Der Liberalismus—eine zeitlose Idee: Nationale, europäische und globale Perspektiven,* ed. G. Habermann and M. Studer (Munich: Olzog Verlag, 2011), 119–30. Reprinted by permission of G. Habermann.

1. Amartya Sen, *The Idea of Justice,* London: Allen Lane, 2009, pp. 12–15.

before we can slice it, somebody must have baked the cake. One theorists postulates that since the status quo is "morally arbitrary," it should be shrouded from our conscience by a veil of ignorance, creating an "original position" where they can agree on a just distribution of all things without knowing whether such a distribution would *give or take* from them some of what is concealed behind the hypothetical veil of ignorance.

Sen is too fine and fastidious an intellect to resort to the crude device of nonowned value. But in his story of the three children quarrelling over the flute, he reduces prior ownership to insignificance.

Carla argues that it was she who made the flute with several months of her own labor, so by rights she should have it. Sen finds that "no-nonsense libertarians" would support her. But why only no-nonsense libertarians? Sen, in an afterthought, adds Marxists, too, on the less than clear ground of labor entitling to ownership.

Be this as it may, the fact is that Carla at present neither possesses nor owns the flute. However, she neither sold nor lost the flute; instead, it was taken from her by the "expropriators." Sen does not say who they were and on what ground they expropriated the flute. If the expropriation was a breach of the rules of justice governing ownership the flute should of course be restored to Carla and everybody, rather than just no-nonsense libertarians and maybe Marxists, should insist on this. Carla should then win the argument against the two other children, not because she has made the flute, but because she owns it by the rules of justice. Before the other two children can expect their arguments for getting the flute to be heard and considered at all, they should first make and win a case for *taking* the flute away from Carla, invalidating the ownership that had been restored to her after the unjust expropriation got corrected. On the other hand, if the expropriation was just, it is now the expropriators who own the flute and the children must first defeat the status quo, i.e., show case for invalidating the ownership of the expropriators, before quarrelling over the flute among themselves.

Though they look crucial to the problem, Sen does not wrestle with these difficulties. He finds it sufficient to establish that thanks to the unidentified expropriators, Carla does not own the flute. Since none of the other children does, they can get on with their dispute and, fortunately for what is to be demonstrated, they do so on an equal footing.

Alone among them, Anne can play the flute. She maintains that she would get more pleasure out of it than the other two and therefore she should get it. Utilitarians hold it to be axiomatic that maximization of pleasure is the criterion of the good, hence they support Anne. They need to be sternly reminded that what is supposed to be maximized is the net balance between pleasure and pain, and that balance must be struck, not for the pleasure and pain of a single plaintiff or supplicant, but for the pleasures and pains of all the different persons who are affected by the decision in favor of or against the plaintiff. We may or may not believe it, but cannot conclusively deny it, that if Anne got the flute, the unhappiness, envy, and frustration of Bob and Carla would be very great, while if she were denied it, Bob and Carla would rub their hands with pleasure that the selfish girl was seen off as she deserved. In other words, the utilitarian, before knowing whom to support, would have to strike an aggregate balance between positive and negative sensations, states of mind, or maybe objective levels of well-being of different persons.

This utilitarian arithmetic was in vogue from the early nineteenth to the mid-twentieth century, and strong residual elements of it often emerge even today in subintellectual political discourse. However, the dominant philosophical view now is that the additions and subtractions of different people's pains and pleasures or "utilities," involving as they do noncommensurate magnitudes, defy logic and are meaningless. Interpersonal comparisons can, of course, be made quite freely, but they must be avowed as personal value judgments of whoever is doing the comparison. Recommendations that Anne should get the flute, no matter how many wise judges would agree with them, cannot claim to be "objective and impartial" because they must rely on evaluations about which bona fide disagreement can never be excluded.

Is Bob's demand to get the flute subject to a similar disability? He is the poorest of the three, and argues that the other two would have enough toys even without the flute, but he would have none. "Economic egalitarians," as Sen calls them, would no doubt support Bob, but would anyone else do so? In the last analysis, egalitarians (no doubt unconsciously and in fond belief) are prisoners of the illusion that "equal" is self-evidently better than "unequal" and should be preferred over an unequal alternative unless a sufficiently strong reason speaks to the contrary. This is a presumption that the egalitarian finds embedded in the very forms of the two words, the second being a denial of the first, coming into its own only after the first is for good reason dismissed.

However, there is no such presumption. To claim that equal is somehow superior to unequal is no more valid than the claim that in like and unlike, like is superior.

In the matter of Bob and the others, flutes and other toys, the only unobjectionable statements are neutral and cut both ways. "Bob should get the flute unless sufficient reasons speak against it," but "Bob should not get the flute unless sufficient reasons are found why he should." The formal equivalence between "he should" and "he should not" gets us precisely nowhere, which is as it should be, for whether a distribution of good or bad things should be equal or unequal cannot be decided on the totally question-begging ground that equal should generally trump unequal. A choice for or against a particular distribution must be made (*if indeed it must be made*) on the relevant evidence and the particular reasons pertaining to the case. Before the reasons are examined, there is no reason whatever to expect the judgment to favor an equal distribution. As there is no presumption either way, the unequal distribution may just as well prove to be the just one. One qualification may be added to this verdict to satisfy the scrupulous, though perhaps it need not be given major significance. This is because there may be reasons why a distribution is what it is without these reasons necessarily being discovered. If revealed, we might deem them good or bad. Our evaluations may be faulty and this source of irreducible uncertainty extends over the whole range of reasons we weigh when trying to decide, if indeed we must, whether Bob should or should not get the flute or, more ambitiously, whether a given distributive status quo should be altered to the profit of some and at the expense of others. This being the case, we may be persuaded to exercise some presumption in favor of the status quo.

To wind up the story of the three children, we must ask whether it is really impossible to find a unifying principle of what Sen calls ideal justice, that would lead straight to the flute being given to one of the children and not to either of the other two.

Neither the utilitarian principle backing Anne's claim nor the egalitarian one pleading for Bob's is solid or difficult for reasonable persons to reject, especially after they are scrutinized with a modicum of rigor. However, it is not the weakness of their internal logic that disqualifies both for the role of sole or dominant principle of justice. It is rather that they are not principles of justice at all. They are features of imaginary societies that appeal to the moral sentiments of many who think that social coexistence could be rendered nicer than it is when pleasures exceed pains, and nicer when nobody is either richer or poorer than anybody else. However, more pleasure than pain, or lesser inequalities, are not matters of justice and it is vain to search among such features for some unifying principle of just arrangements.

Out of the arguments advocating alternative assignments of the flute, only the one favoring Carla is an argument of, and from, justice. The reason she should have the flute is not, as Sen suggests, that she has made it with her own labor (though disciples of Locke would think so). The reason rather is that she is the presumptive owner. She was the possessor of the flute; there was no known reason for doubting her title to it; she was dispossessed by the "expropriators," but there is no known reason for holding that they had a stronger claim to it; therefore, as far as is known, she is still the owner and the flute should in justice be restored to her.

Pace Sen, this is not a "no-nonsense libertarian" conclusion. It is the conclusion of all who play by the rules and look for an answer in justice, and not in niceness.

PROPERTY, LIBERTY, AND THE AMBIGUITY OF RIGHTS

There is a theory both of the narrow concept of the social order, namely property, and of the broader one, liberty, that is simpler and makes a lesser demand on our credulity and wishful thinking than any other habitually cited. Its basic building block is the Nash equilibrium, in which individuals spontaneously coordinate their conduct with one another in such a way that neither party to an interaction can unilaterally increase his advantage ("payoff") derived from it. An interaction offers the possibility of two or more (pure or mixed-strategy) equilibria. Conduct settles on one, hopefully nearer the higher than the lower end of the range of mutual advantages produced by the range of possible equilibria. The one selected partly by luck and partly by deliberate search for reciprocity of behavior becomes a convention, enforced by the threat of retaliation or other social sanctions. The passage of time refines and consolidates conventions into rules. Some have their origins in distant prehistory; others are more recent. There is sufficient empirical evidence of their existence, and their survival beneath subsequent layers of nonspontaneous, collectively decided legislation testifies to their durability and the social mechanisms that enforce them.

Hume, the first major thinker explicitly to recognize the presence and nature of conventional rules, singled out three for special mention: they ensure "the stability of possession, its translation by consent and the keeping of promises." They were "antecedent to government." Unowned resources become owned property by "first possession,"[2] by such interactions as first come, first served and finders, keepers. Property is respected by nonowners obeying the rule that reflects the equilibrium of mutual advantage. It may be transferred to others by inheritance, gift, or exchange, the last including nonsimultaneous execution (credit) made practicable by the rule of promise-keeping (notably, the performance of contracts).

This theory of the incentive-based origins of property is ascertainable, demanding no belief in moral intuition or the ordering hand of government. Sufficient evidence from anthropology and social history testifies to it.

Conventions to yield mutual advantage by banning wrongs do not stop at the wrongs to property, such as trespass, usurpation, theft, default, and fraud. With greater or lesser stringency, they reach out to all wrongs that may arise in social coexistence, ranging from killing or maiming to interference with the pursuit of the peaceful purposes of others. Bad-neighborliness, nuisances (including pollution), and incivilities are objects of more recent or less strict rules.

The set of our feasible actions is thus divided in two. A subset is selected as wrong and banned by spontaneous rules. The nonbanned complement of the set, that is, the entire residual universe of feasible acts, is free. The theory of liberty and of justice stripped of rhetoric is a

2. David Hume, *A Treatise of Human Nature,* Oxford: Clarendon Press, 1978, p. 541.

theory of rules. Perfect liberty, unalloyed by metarules of authority, is defined by spontaneously adopted rules alone. The theory of property from this perspective turns out to be a special case of the more general theory of liberty. Succinctly, property is a liberty.

This is not what mainstream political theory teaches today. It tells us instead that property is a right, that there are property rights conferred by society, that they are assigned, that there are rights to liberties codified by bills of rights, and that the first principle of justice is that everybody must have a right to the greatest possible system of liberties. What, if anything, is the word "right" doing here that would not be done without it? and if it is not an irrelevance, where does it come from and what is its force?

In properly used language, a right has meaning only in an implied conjunction with a matching obligation. The right holder has the option to exercise it by requiring the obligor to perform a defined act (I have a right to his performance) or not to perform one (I have a right to his forbearance). The obligation is a sham, and so is the right, if the obligor was in any case rule-bound to do or not to do what the right supposedly requires him to do or not to do. "I have a right that all respect my home" is a sham right if all must respect my home anyway, and never mind my right.

Rights and the matching obligations are created voluntarily by agreement (including its reciprocal form, the contract), or by authority with powers to confer a right and impose the obligation. It is not clear how else rights originate and the language which treats them is charged with ambiguity.

Grasping the differences between a theater, a church, and a nunnery is not hard; nor should the one between a right and a liberty be beyond common comprehension. If you bought a ticket, you have a right to come and see the play and the theater manager is obliged to put it on. When a church is open, you are free to enter. It makes no sense to say that you have a right to this freedom. A nunnery is closed to men except to the nuns' confessor and the physician. It is not that they have a right that other men do not; it is that the rules governing access to the nunnery leave them free.

The Bill of Rights states that you (and all others similarly placed) have a right to free speech. However, gagging is intrinsically wrong and is banned, quite regardless of whether it violates your right to free speech. Giving you a right purporting to protect you from wrongs impairing your speech is giving you something you already have.

GIFTS OF RIGHTS

There may or may not be a unifying principle of justice that dominates others in shaping the social order, but men usually believe in one, particularly in retrospect. Thus, the Christian era until the eighteenth century was understood to see ideal order in Natural Law. Natural Law was a corollary of natural rights whose source was the divine purpose that God destines for man. This is an adequate foundation for rights provided the belief is uncontested. As religious belief faded, man's purpose and his natural rights faded with it. The Enlightenment put a more or less clearly defined Reason in the position of supreme ordering principle. With hindsight, it was predictable that utilitarianism would be its successor. After a reign that wrought a quite fundamental change in the political arrangements of the Western world, utilitarianism went into steep decline. By the mid-twentieth century, such ideas as the "separateness of individuals" and "man must not be a means" came to be widely voiced. The doctrine starting with Bentham and ending with Pigou and the "social welfare function" was being kicked when it was already down. Rights, sometimes embellished to become "human rights" or "social rights," became the dominant idea in political thought.

Unlike natural rights before their source dried out, secular rights have the curious characteristic that they have no visible or even particularly plausible source. They rest on one of two assertions. One is, as Robert Nozick audaciously put it in the starting sentence of his chief book, that "Individuals have rights."[3] This is an arbitrary statement and though we may agree to it, there is no reason why we should. The rights so affirmed have no identifiable source. Alternatively, it may be held that in a well-ordered society, individuals ought to have an array of rights. They may actually have some of these, but if they lack others, something should be done to remedy the insufficiency. Within the "rightsism" that characterizes current political theory and discourse,

3. Robert Nozick, *Anarchy, State, and Utopia,* Oxford: Blackwell, 1974, p. ix.

it is not always clear which of these two senses the word is meant to convey. What is clear throughout, however, is that no attention at all is paid to whether the right in question is genuine, i.e., ready to be exercised at the rightholder's option thanks to the existence of a matching obligation, or spurious because no matching obligation exists that would enable the right holder to exercise it. In the latter case, instead of using a spurious concept, it would be more telling and also more honest to speak, not of rights, but of aspirations we share, approve in others, and endeavor to transform into realizable options, though such goals may be out of reach for the time being.

However, it may well be that the force of rightsism resides precisely in this dishonesty. Rightsism *gives* without *taking*, or at least without taking visibly. It confers rights (or confirms that they exist) without at the same time imposing the obligations that would make these rights into real ones. Such gifts of rights are irresistibly attractive to anyone who is even a shade gullible. They have become the standard currency of practical politics. The gift raises expectations, which will either turn out to be false and turn into angry, pressing claims, or else they are gradually and partially satisfied by the a posteriori imposition of obligations. The practical upshot is a tendency for welfare states to expand into a fiscal danger zone in which indebtedness gets out of control and the distribution of income between generations shifts in a way nobody really intended.

It is worth noting that the nineteenth-century precursors of rightsism, the American Bill of Rights and the French Declaration of the Rights of Man and Citizen, do not hand out gifts in the above sense. They merely proclaim rights to an itemized list of freedoms that are considered more important than the myriad other freedoms not figuring on the list. The present paper argues that a right to a liberty is a wellhead from which confused thought gushes and spreads out to contaminate commonsense understanding.

Commonsense understanding takes us to rules that separate the set of feasible acts into a part that is banned and a residual one that is left free. The rule-abiding individual chooses to perform acts belonging to this residual universe. The acts are freedoms by definition and it is oxymoronic to say that he has a right to perform them. It might be thought, though, that the matter is not as simple as that, for what if the individual is prevented, by force or the threat of force, from performing a certain act that the rules leave free? Would that not violate his right? The answer, of course, is that whoever was doing the forcible interference with his freedom, whether it was a rogue individual or a rogue state, would be breaching the rules and this would be a wrong, regardless of whether or not our individual had a right to perform the act in question. This is the case if the rules in force ("the rule of law") are beyond question, separating the banned from the free not only in the de facto, but also in some normative sense. Interestingly, the 1789 French Declaration of the Rights of Man and Citizen fails to grasp this point; in Article 4 it states that the rights it declares are in effect subordinated to the existing legal order (hence they cannot be contesting it) and this limitation renders them redundant.

It is possible, and all too often true, that the legal order bans as unfree a range of acts that many of us would judge as deserving to be left free. Does that mean that we have "rights" to them? Lack of unanimity about an act deserving to be treated as a freedom cannot be resolved by rhetoric and the solemnity of proclamations. There is one objective test that minimizes the role of persuasion and moral sentiments: it is whether liberation of the act would generate additional mutual advantage. We may reasonably hold that if it would add to net mutual advantage, it would at least potentially be protected by the system of spontaneous rules. The legal rule suppressing it would then be a wrong, a destroyer of mutual advantage. However, to declare that we have a right not to be subjected to such a legal rule would be saying no more than that we ought not to be wronged. Assuming a right, namely, that we must have a right not to be wronged, would be redundant at best, asinine by slightly more exacting standards.

If having a right to freedom means all freedoms excluding none (which the U.S. Bill of Rights professes to do, warning us that addressing a list of freedoms does not imply neglect of those not on the list), "we have a right to all the freedoms" would be synonymous with "all freedoms are free," hardly an exciting tautology.

However, if a bill of rights necessarily implies that the freedoms not inventoried in the bill differ from those that are (though it may be unclear in exactly what way they differ), a bill of rights takes a good part of the road toward a truly ominous split of the presumption of liberty into two contradictory versions. It used to be said that one version defined the general attitude to liberty west of the river Elbe, the other east of it. The world west of the Elbe held to the presumption that "everything is free that is not prohibited," while that east of the Elbe accepted that "everything that is not stated to be free is prohibited." West of the Elbe prohibitions were itemized and the nonitemized residual universe was left free. East of the Elbe, freedoms were itemized (and were perceived as permissions), and the residual universe became unfree by implication. It is no doubt inexact to have the two contrary presumptions coincide with geographical areas. Both can be found both in the West and in the East. Some observers would contend that in both West and East, the drift of political thought toward rightsism is crowding out the presumption that all is free unless explicitly ruled out, and is eagerly making more room for the presumption that free is what we get explicit rights to, with the rest ranging from the dubious and uncertain to the prohibited.

Here, we are no longer dealing with the misuse of language, but with its sinister consequences that show why we should not dismiss the misuse with a shrug.

Rightsism distributes gifts with both hands. One bestows freedoms; we have just been looking at them. The other hands out rights to goods and services that are mostly sham rights not matched by the corresponding obligations; the *giving* is displayed, but the *taking* that the exercise of these putative rights would require is passed over in silence.

The 1948 Declaration of Human Rights of the United Nations, the first in a series of proclamations and charters, serves as a classic example. In its preamble, it fixes the double goal of securing rights to two freedoms, one of the freedom from fear, the other from want. The freedom from fear must relieve anxiety about the stability of rules that secure liberty by banning wrongdoing, including wrongdoing by governments. The rules are presumably made safe by declaring that we have a right to the freedoms they secure. Freedom from want, in turn, is offered in the form of another type of proclaimed rights to a sufficiency of goods and services. Various rights assure this directly or indirectly. Article 24, for instance, states that we have a right to work, which the article interprets as a right to gainful employment on agreeable terms, consistent with human dignity and permitting human development. No one is designated as responsible for offering this gainful employment on such conditions, though mention is made of the efforts of national governments and of international cooperation in the service of this end. The article leaves its reader wondering whether it was hypocrisy, cynicism, or just plain woolly thinking that mainly inspired this text.

In fairness, it must be added that in the postwar crop of international manifestos of rights there are elements that do impose obligations on consenting governments to satisfy the proclaimed rights. This is the case with the 1950 European Convention that binds the signatory governments in some matters concerning individual immunities ("civil liberties"). It is particularly the case with the Charter of Fundamental Rights in the aborted European constitution, which was reborn as an annex of the Lisbon Treaty into which it found its way through the back door. This Charter declares "social" or workers' rights which national governments are supposed to enforce as obligations of employers. The rights created by these treaty instruments are not sham. However, their exercise provokes inconsistencies with policies on illegal immigration and antiterrorist controls. Enforcement of "social" rights renders labor markets dysfunctional, damages the very worker interests it tries to protect, and contributes to an expansion of the welfare state that the economy can ultimately not sustain and that benefits nobody. In this context, gifts of spurious rights may prove less harmful than gifts of real ones.

REFERENCES

Hume, D. 1978. *A Treatise of Human Nature.* Oxford: Clarendon Press.

Nozick, R. 1974. *Anarchy, State, and Utopia.* Oxford: Blackwell.

Sen, A. 2009. *The Idea of Justice.* London: Allen Lane.

4. HUMAN RIGHTS AND WRONGS
MISNOMERS, ILLUSIONS, TENSIONS

Why must you not kill any stranger you may casually meet? Two alternative answers suggest themselves, one referring to rights, the other to rules. The choice depends on what we understand society's dominant organizing principle ought to be, but also on which principle appears to be feasible and, if both are, which one is prevalent as a matter of ascertainable fact. The "rights or rules" question seems to be largely open and serves as the underlying theme of this paper, while its focus is on the particular notion of human rights.

RIGHTS OR RULES?

If one agrees to the postulate that people have a right to live, killing any one of them is a violation of both his right and the right to life in general. Rights violations are wrong by definition and no wrongs must be done.

Some very strong reasons for killing may override the right to life, though obviously none could be held against a casual stranger. The violation of the right to life itself could arguably justify killing a murderer, but the problem of reasons strong enough to override the right to life must be left for another occasion.

Two considerations occur to render the rights-based deduction precarious. First, the postulate that there is a right to live, being metaphysical and having no truth value, must rely on intuitive appeal, but its appeal is limited (though it is perhaps the best in the great panoply of human rights). A postulate like "it is wrong to kill" appears to have stronger intuitive appeal. Second, if reliance is placed on the more direct postulate that killing is wrong *an sich* the rights-based reason for not killing people becomes "people have a right not to be *wronged*"

Previously unpublished; © 2015 by Liberty Fund, Inc.

which is both analytic and silly; it is wrong to be wronged whether we have rights or not.

How does the rule-based reason for not killing casual strangers compare? When mutual killing is unrestrained, life is "nasty, brutish, solitary, and short." The payoffs of players in the "game of life" are at their minimum. There is equilibrium, as no player can increase his payoff by unilaterally changing his behavior. They are all on the lowest rung of a sort of ladder, with each higher rung standing for a behavior where mutual killing is less frequent. Each rung up on the ladder corresponds to a progressively higher game sum and potentially higher payoffs to each player (though the distribution of the game sum among the players is left open). On the top rung where nobody kills anybody, mutual advantage is at its maximum. On any intermediate rung, a player may quit the equilibrium and step onto a higher rung, i.e., behave more peacefully, in the hope of reciprocity by the other player(s). If the response to his initiative (which is not foreseen in classical game theory) is indeed reciprocal, a new equilibrium of coordination is established on the higher rung. Successively higher equilibria may spontaneously emerge in an evolutionary process. A high equilibrium (but not necessarily the potential maximum or the Pareto-optimum) is a convention involving a strategy conditional on reciprocity in coordination. The convention imperceptibly solidifies into a rule.

Under the conventional rule, wrong is what obstructs or destroys mutual advantage. In addition to killing, most if not all torts have a payoff structure that rewards reciprocally "nice" behavior by greater mutual advantage. Among these, the respect for property and the keeping of promises play a key role and were recognized and emphasized by Hume. Similar, though perhaps somewhat weaker, incentive structures explain conventional rules against nuisances and incivilities.

Unlike the handful of "pure" conventions that are perfectly self-enforcing, most of the conventions that interest us are enforcement-dependent. The player who breaks the rule is punished in a great variety of ways by other players. The risk of punishment must weigh sufficiently to spoil the free-rider payoff the breaking of the rule would otherwise yield, for otherwise rule breaking would become too frequent for the convention to survive. Unlike the rights-based reason for a desired social organization that depends on affirmations about rights that may but need not be believed and that, as will be argued in the latter part of this paper, generate conflict rather than mutual advantage, the rule-based organization is a matter of historical fact going back a very long way. It is not a matter of belief or of aspiration. Moreover, it is driven by an incentive structure involving mutual advantage that could be expected to bring about the very same result that we do in fact find.

"RIGHTSISM" AND THE ADVENT OF HUMAN RIGHTS

The very distinct weakness of a rights-based theory in both the normative and the positive mode notwithstanding, modern social thought has come to be centrally occupied by rights. The rhetoric that accompanies actual policy is also richly embellished by them. Perhaps because of some doubt whether these rights mean the same thing and do the same service as the rights people exercise when they are calling in the debts others owe to them, the newly canvassed rights are now often called "human rights." Adding the adjective subtly shifts the meaning away from the original, though it takes some thought to understand in quite what way the shift goes. (Much the same shift takes place when the adjective "social" is added to justice.) In subsequent sections, I shall occasionally speak of "aspirations" instead of "human rights" in order to serve as a reminder that these "human" rights are not rights in the ordinary sense.

From the Enlightenment to about the mid-twentieth century, utilitarianism was the dominant normative standard of the good society. Its pain-and-pleasure calculus, its objective of satisfaction, preference-fulfillment, and the rational pursuit thereof by individuals, brought it the support of economics, whose manner of reasoning made natural allies of the two. Jointly, they provided the intellectual inspiration of policy. The recognition that different persons' satisfactions, their gains or losses, are not commensurate; that they cannot be added to or subtracted from one another; and that "the greatest happiness of the greatest number" is just gibber-jabber, discredited utilitarianism and also much of welfare economics. Socialism, contradicting some deep-seated utilitarian ideals, was unsuited to fill the gap left by the latter's demise. Strongly favored by the postwar zeitgeist, "rightsism" rapidly filled the vacuum.

It seems to me important to say at this juncture that the "right" of modern "rightsism" is not a direct descendant of the medieval Thomist and even Hobbesian notion of a law of nature, willed by God, into which man fits so as to fulfill the purpose God designed for him. It is man's divine purpose that calls for natural rights as its *enabling conditions,* defining what he must be able to do and what must not be done to him. There is, in my view, no evident continuity between this religious metaphysics and the secular metaphysics of contemporary "rightsism," which ascribes rights to man's dignity or is content blankly to declare, as does Robert Nozick in the opening sentence of his *Anarchy, State, and Utopia,* that "Individuals have rights." Maybe dignity is an adequate progenitor of rights, though maybe it is not. Maybe man has dignity, but maybe he has not. Maybe animals, plants, and inanimate artefacts also have dignity, though maybe they do not. Maybe dignity is not necessary to have rights; it is sufficient for people to exist and the same might well be true of animals, plants, and works of art. However, the contrary may also be true. Evidently, the very discussion is infantile and supports one position no better than its opposite; any conclusion that might stop it can only be an arbitrary assertion nobody is bound to accept.

If so, something must be wrong with "rightsism" and its central subject, human rights.

A PURGE OF MISUSED WORDS

A person is "under an obligation" if another person can require him to perform a defined act that he would be at liberty not to perform if he were not under the obligation. Symmetrically, a person is under an obligation if another person can require him to forbear from performing an act that he would otherwise be at liberty to perform. The person who can so require him is said to have the right to do so; he is the right holder, while the counterparty whom he has the right to require to act or to forbear from acting is the obligor. The right holder is exercising his right when he requires the obligor to act, or to forbear from acting.

A right that cannot be exercised is not a real right. At best, it is an expectation of one (e.g., a deferred right) or an aspiration to acquire one. At worst, it is an illusion, a deceit, a false promise, a fraud.

Real rights are created in two ways. One is to acquire a right by contract; the other is to have it conferred by an authority having the competence to do so. A typical example of contract is the contract of exchange, where one party promises to deliver a good or service against payment, while the other party promises to pay against the delivery of a good or service. Each party is both a right holder and an obligor. (A unilateral promise by a promisor involving no consideration in return by the promisee is not generally regarded as creating a right.) Alternatively, a right may be conferred on one person in conjunction with the imposition upon another person of a matching obligation. Though it should go without saying, it is perhaps worth spelling out that the contracted right meets the incentives of both parties; the conferred right goes against those of the obligor, and must involve the threat of coercion by the authority that imposes it. Contracted rights arise spontaneously; conferred ones do not. Partisans of the political authority regularly disguise the implied coercion and dress up these rights as voluntary by claiming that there exists a social contract, universally agreed to, by which potential obligors, e.g., the well-to-do, have in advance consented to the obligations that are imposed upon them. This, then, may supposedly give the same incentive-compatible result indirectly that the voluntary rights-creating contract gives directly.

It is a misuse of language to call "right" something that is not a real right. We cannot very well call them "unreal rights." A radical purge of misused words may not be practicable. Adding a qualifying adjective as in "human rights," though mitigating the linguistic abuse, injects an element of confusion of meaning. Although it might seem unduly rigorous and purist to insist on avoiding it, nevertheless use of the term "rights" where there are none is to condone and favor a potentially dangerous misnomer and perhaps fraud.

A right cannot be exercised and hence it is not a real right if it is not bound to a matching obligation. An obligation, in turn, is not credible and may be a fake unless a clearly defined obligor is liable to carry it out. "It is society's duty to ensure that civil rights are respected" is very far from securing the exercise of civil rights by all who are said to have them.

There is one other constantly recurring configuration where the use of the word "right" is a misnomer: it is when the right, even if it existed, need not be exercised because a liberty makes it redundant. Consider our often and loudly asserted "right" of dissent: "I have a right to criticize the government, or isn't this a free country?" Since "free country" presumably implies freedom to criticize the government, you may go ahead and do it without having to claim your right to require an obstructive obligor to let you do it. If he tries to obstruct you, he must be violating the public order that delineates what is free from what is not. Likewise, if others are not at liberty to dispossess you, it is a misnomer to speak of your "property *right*" instead of your property. If others are not free to dispossess you, your property is one of your liberties, and not one of your rights. The improper use of the word "right" in this context has, in fact, a subtle but significant effect on ideology and politics. (The term "property rights" is not a misnomer when it denotes relations derived from property, e.g., owner-tenant, creditor-debtor, insurer-insured, shareholder, option giver and taker, etc.) The difference between property and its derivatives is relevant to whether property is a product of the legal order or, as Hume emphasized, prior to it. Therefore, wiping out the difference by redundant and even pompous references to "property rights" when we mean simply "property" is potentially poisonous.

Statesmen, politicians running for office, and writers in economics and politics, all prolific users and misusers of the ideas and the words "right" and "human rights," are not the only ones to confuse who owes and who owns, who may and who must, what is optional and what is obligatory. Ordinary speech by ordinary people is also in need of a purge by a dose of plain common sense. People under contract to work for an employer must get up early on weekdays to go to their place of work. The employer has a right to require them and they are obliged to comply. However, when they get up at noon on a Sunday, they are apt to explain the self-indulgence by saying that they have a *right* to stay in bed as long as they like on a Sunday. What they have is of course a *liberty* and not a right: the liberty that is very clearly defined by the absence of any constraint. Since there is no rule against getting up later on Sundays or an obligation to get up early, one is at liberty to get up late. Calling this liberty a *right* suggests that the speaker feels he lives in an environment of universal constraint where any act requires a right to perform it, for "everything is prohibited unless it is specifically permitted." Who, anyway, confers the right? Every time one of us says, "It is my right to . . ." when he ought to be saying "I am free to . . . ," he fosters a climate of constraint where a right to do is needed, though the absence of a rule against doing suffices.

It is thus that "rightsism," intended to affirm freedom and autonomy, makes for dependence on putative rights and on those who hold the power and authority to proclaim them and confer them.

SAYING SO WON'T MAKE IT SO

The Preamble of the 1948 Declaration of Human Rights of the United Nations states that its object is to assert the imprescriptible right of everyone to freedom from *fear* and *want.* The two key words correspond to the broad division rightsism often makes between so-called "negative" and "positive" rights. Disregarding for the moment the objectionable formula of a "right to freedom," arguably an oxymoron, as well as the term "negative" right which is no less so, we may take it that the intended division refers to rights not to be wronged, i.e., that certain inadmissible acts must not be done to you, and on the other hand to rights to do and obtain certain things that relieve you from want.

I have argued in Section 1 that if something is defined as *wrong,* it must not be done. It is nonsensical to claim a right that it should not be done to you or anyone who has this right, since we have also said that it must not be done anyway, right or no right. The "right to freedom from fear" boils down to a definition of what the wrongs are that are feared and must not be done, and how the interdiction of such things is enforced.

The 1789 French Declaration of the Rights of Man and Citizen, behind its verbiage about rights, makes it quite clear that the real content is limited to this definition. Article 2 states that "the natural and imprescriptible rights of man . . . are Liberty, Property, Safety and Resistance to Oppression." Article 4 adds: ". . . the exercise of the natural right of every man has . . . bounds (that) may be determined only by law." In other words, it is the rules in force that determine what you are permitted or are at liberty to do and what others are at liberty to do to you. Once the set of liberties is so defined, "freedom from fear" is implicit in the definition, at least as regards any fear of others doing rule-breaking things to you. These things naturally include things your own government could do to you if it broke the rules. Rights have nothing to do with it; inserting them is double-counting. Moreover, what is being enforced is the "law." He who proclaims that "we have rights" is saying no more than that "rules are enforced" or, in more traditional language, that "we have freedom under the rule of law." A corollary of this is that it is false to proclaim that the unfortunate denizens of the Third World who live under barbarous and corrupt regimes and not under the rule of law "have human rights." They do not. They may have aspirations, and we may heartily wish them success. But we should eschew language that confounds wishes and realities.

Much the same goes, though perhaps even more acutely, for the "right to freedom from want." The "fear" in the freedom from "fear" is evidently confined to the wrongs others are not permitted to do to you. The "freedom from want" and the oxymoronic "right" to it, however, appear to be limited only by the riches of the pompous vocabulary that describes all the good things the United Nations, the 1950 European Convention on Human Rights, or the Lisbon Treaty declares that we are entitled to.

No benevolent uncle, no vote-seeking politician could be more thoughtful in taking into account all the wants we may have and more generous in listing all the good things they not only wish us to have but that by virtue of our human rights we must be able to get. Article 22 of the U.N. 1948 proclamation states: "Everyone . . . has the right to social security, and is entitled to realization, through national effort . . . of the economic and social rights indispensable for his dignity and free development of his personality." Article 23 continues: "Everyone has the right to work, to free choice of employment, to just and favorable conditions of work . . ." In Article 26, we are assured that "Everyone has a right to education. Elementary education shall be compulsory." (In the Lisbon Treaty, the corresponding article declares that everyone has the *right* to *compulsory* education!) No rights to a sufficiency of food and to adequate housing are separately conferred. But by exercising the right to favorable employment, one can no doubt take care of the want of food and shelter as well.

While voluble on rights, the United Nations is silent on who is obliged to provide the social security, the education, and the desirable employment when humanity tries to exercise the rights it was given to these good things. There is a discreet allusion to national effort and international cooperation, two meaningless platitudes that commit nobody to anything. The rights enumerated here are of course empty humbug because no obligors are designated to provide the means permitting their exercise. It might be thought that since many hundreds of millions in the developed parts of the world are in just and favorable conditions of employment and free from basic wants, rightsism does work after all and human rights are not unreal. But this, alas, is not the relevant empirical test. The test is whether the putative right holder, if in want of the good things his human dignity entitles him to have, has a known and identifiable person or group that is obliged to respond to his call and lift him out of his misery. This test is negative. Succour may come from goodwill and charity, but no one has a right to that. Goodwill and charity are moral duties, and not contracted or imposed obligations. Succour of a sort may also come from the welfare state caught up in the mechanics of political competition for support. Even hardened hypocrites would hesitate to pretend that this is done in obedience to human rights.

ASK FOR THE MOON

Rightsism in general and human rights talk in particular confidently display a lack of command of logic and language of which even mediocre schoolboys should blush. This may well worry those, such as the present author, who believe that misuse and abuse of language, fudge and willingness are slow-acting but very vicious poison in the body politic. Others who regard sloppy language as at worst a peccadillo, may nevertheless fear the influence of the relentless human rights talk that surrounds us. The false promises, the pressing solicitations that "here is nothing, hold hard onto it," the illusions that solemn proclamations by august institutions must be worth something, can hardly fail to impact the public mind. Disappointment, frustration, and mistrust are the likely results. Demands for redistribution are apt to be more peremptory when inspired not only by plain interest, but also by a righteous belief in human rights being on one's side. Instead of standards of justice and conciliatory agreement, human rights are apt to be sources of tension.

Can we nevertheless find them endowed with a saving grace? I believe they do have one, though whether it is strong enough to earn them absolution for their vices against common sense and realism is not certain. Insistent talk about human rights bears some resemblance to the age-old bargaining practice of asking for the moon. It is not a sure and safe tactic, for it may cut off negotiation before it can really start. Sometimes, however, asking for the moon does get you the earth.

Where this has a chance of working and doing some good is in international relations with states not willing or incapable of upholding the rule of law. Their governments are cruel and incompetent criminal associations and kleptocracies that do great wrong to their peoples by sheer irresponsibility if not by deliberate design. Almost without exception, however, their ruling elites desperately crave respect and recognition as members of a legitimate upper set, what the French would call *frequentable* and the Germans *salonfähig*. Hearing incantations about human rights and being accused of violating them is a source of some unease and discomfort when these people travel to rich and civilized capitals, meet their opposite numbers, risk their wives being snubbed in fashionable society and themselves pilloried in press and television. They will pay lip service to human rights while claiming that such rights are sacred back home, as any "objective" observer must acknowledge. Little by little, they may even make concessions to pacify the observers and earn themselves a better press.

None of this will give the whole earth to those who ask for the moon, but it is not worthless either. Dumb tyrannies usually perish by starting to make small concessions. All the false human rights discourse may be forgiven if it nudges vicious states a little toward some such destiny.

PART 3

Contractarianism and Its Surroundings

1. CONDUCT AND CONTRACT

INTRODUCTION

Though even large agglomerations of people manage to live together in some semblance of mostly peaceful order, it is not really evident why they succeed in doing so. Hobbes held that the obvious presumption was that of "warre" and that some artefact, typically a Leviathan (Hobbes 1968 [1651]), needed to be grafted on to formless agglomerations of men to overcome the presumed condition of "warre" and create a society out of the state of nature. Prior to Hobbes, no such presumption was generally accepted, while post-Hobbes, explaining the near-miracle of an orderly society has been and might well remain a central preoccupation of social philosophy.

Two theories with a claim to being sufficient explanations are the front-runners. In one, the work of establishing and maintaining a viable order is done by spontaneously arising conventions, in the other by consciously agreed obligations that have the appearance of a social contract. It is not really asserted that a social contract has in fact been concluded in times past (though an apocryphal history of Venice does assert it), but only that the result is one that we would expect a social contract to produce if it had been concluded. Adding a belt to the braces, it is also pointed out that though no contract may have been actually concluded, their need for one would have induced a people in the state of nature to enter into one. Both the first or "as if" and the second or hypothetical version could be admitted in place of the historically real one provided the idea of a social contract was agreed as compatible with plausible notions of rationality.

Thanks to the increasing interest in Hume in the last few decades, the nature and role of conventions is now widely understood. They are forms of conduct that, if adopted by a significant number of people, yield enhanced benefits to each; hence, if a critical threshold number

From *RMM* (*Rationality, Markets and Morals: Studies at the Intersection of Philosophy and Economics*), ed. Max Albert, Hartmut Kliemt, and Bernd Lahno, 4 (2013): 53–60. *http://www.rmm-journal.de/*. Reprinted by permission.

adheres to a convention, nonadherents are induced to adhere. Doing so is not the result of agreement, but is a unilateral choice. All conventions are (Nash) equilibria (see Lewis 1969), i.e., self-enforcing, but only a few are self-enforcing in the simple sense that deviation from them is ipso facto bad for the deviant; language, paper money, and the rule of the road are well-known examples of the simple ones. Most conventions, however, are self-enforcing only in a composite sense: they leave a free rider option open to the deviant, but trigger off a punishment strategy if he attempts to take advantage of it by actually deviating. A wide range of punishments is available to deter free riding. Refusal to interact with the deviant in a significant number of future rounds of the "game" is perhaps the most obvious one, but of course there are others. It must be assumed that the cost of punishment is no greater than the advantage of suppressing free riding and thus protecting the convention from unravelling and favoring its longevity. Some such assumption does not look unreasonable, for it explains the timeless survival of conventions that seem to invite free riding. Let us note that no central, specialized enforcer seems necessary or even economical, especially as the employment of one (e.g., Nozick's "protective agency" that ultimately leads to the formation of the state, see Nozick 1974) creates principal-agent problems that are liable to occasion very high costs indeed in exploitation and loss of freedoms.

A Humean system of conventions may consist of three tiers. The most important works against torts; it protects life and limb, the free pursuit of peaceful purposes, in Hume's words "the stability of possession" (Hume 1978, Book III, Part II, Sect. 3) and their "transference by consent" (Sect. 4) as well as the keeping of promises (Sect. 5). In the second tier there are conventions against nuisances and negative externalities. In our day, some new conventions against environmental degradation may come to be added to the other externalities of this second tier, though it is too early to be sure. The third tier of only loosely enforced conventions work against incivilities and defend some amenities of civilization.

The set of these conventions, tolerably well adhered to but not necessarily seamless, looks comfortably sufficient to create and uphold a social order that can tellingly be called ordered anarchy. On thorough consideration, the set is adequate to induce what should be called just conduct on the part of enough members of society for there to be a high degree of justice and freedom. On the other hand, ordered anarchy offers no mechanism enabling nonunanimous collective choices to be made and for politics to take hold—a systemic shortcoming that some of us may regard as a safeguard and a benefaction.

It is perhaps worth adding that all well-established conventions qualify to be treated as rules made by use without being derived from any higher, rule-making rule. The essential ones may also be regarded as moral rules in that they act to defeat indisputable wrongs. It may even be tenable to hold that such conventions alone qualify as moral rules.

MORAL CONTRACTARIANISM

Showing that individual maximization of potentially available advantages entails a social order we might call ordered anarchy made up of spontaneously emerging conventions of just conduct, leaves us free to propose that some of these conventions rise to the rank of moral rules that function as such, in that they constrain choices because they are taboo and not because they maximize the exploitation of available advantages, though they continue to do that, too. This would amount to saying that honesty is the best policy, but the rules of just conduct induce individuals to act honestly regardless of the advantage they derive from doing so. If this proposition has merit, it is that it is harmless and undemanding, leaving little or no work left for Occam's razor to do.

One major alternative to ordered anarchy is contractarianism that, unlike anarchy, is said to depend on agreement. In its most prominent versions, a basic assumption (the veil of uncertainty in Buchanan 1975, the veil of ignorance in Rawls 1971) molds preferences in such a way that all wish to live in a society of qualified egalitarianism. However, they need no agreement, let alone a contract, in order to do so. Any binding commitment is redundant and the term "contractarian" looks a misnomer.

A less easily comprehended theory, libelled as moral contractarianism, is one mainly associated with the name of David Gauthier (1986). Stripped to its essentials, it seems to be saying that in some initial status quo, individuals follow practices that constrain "direct" maximization for the very good reason that if they did not respect certain constraints, the reactions of counterparties to the attempted unconstrained maximization would result in a worse outcome than constrained maximization. It turns out, however, that potentially there exists a different set of practices that is superior to the one actually in use. While the actual constrained practice is a Pareto-improvement over "direct" maximization, the potentially superior practice is actually Pareto-optimal. Though it is not easy to feel confident when trying to fathom Gauthier's meaning, it would seem that it is their Pareto-optimality that leads him to accord moral character to these superior practices, and it is mutual agreement that enables them to be attained and maintained.

The well-known Folk Theorem (Fudenberg and Maskin 1986) makes an incontrovertible case for holding that interactions of the prisoners' dilemma type, not adopting the dominant (direct-maximizing) strategy, can yield any number of superior payoffs if the players expect the interaction to be repeated; there is no telling which of these potentially superior equilibrium strategies will in fact be adopted. Over a much broader range of types of interactions, the Humean theory of conventions is telling us the same thing. The equilibria in these conventions are Pareto-improving, but may or may not be Pareto-optimal. Nor do we have any supplementary theory of a mechanism that would lead to Panglossian Pareto-optimality. Neither the Folk Theorem nor the broader set of Humean conventions depends on agreement of any sort. They obviously depend on expectations of the responses of others to our own strategies, but this is not agreement, not even a tacit one, about the strategies the parties would commit themselves to in order to reach the putative optimum. Neither such negotiation nor the commitment to it is easy to imagine in real life. The least demanding theory would assume that Pareto-optimum is possible and if reached, it could have been reached by negotiated agreement and commitment. Perhaps this is how we should treat Gauthier's theory, though he seems to demand far more for "deliberative rationality" to accomplish.

If the claim that optimality can be reliably reached is abandoned—a claim I think is particular to Gauthier—we are left with a general contractarian claim that agreement leads to mutual advantage. It is easy enough to sustain that agreement; a quasi-contract (hence the name "contractarianism," presumably as distinct from "social contract theory") is a sufficient condition for generating improved outcomes. It seems to me more difficult to sustain that it is a necessary condition. The supposition that people need to agree to do what they wish to do is redundant. Note in this context that insofar as Buchanan's and Rawls's version of contractarianism involves redistribution of society's goods, they represent this as the unanimous wish of the citizenry. For agreeing to do what one wishes to do, without stating the redundant, a stress must be laid on the meaning and nature of cooperation that I think it should not be asked to bear.

Consider the case of two men Will and John who both want to cross a river. Will has a boat and John has a pair of oars. I believe they would without further ado get into the boat and row across without previous agreement about taking turns at rowing and the fee John would pay Will for using the boat and Will would pay John for using the oars. As to agreement about sharing the fruit of their cooperation, Nature has already allotted the shares: Will has his "utility" gained by reaching the shore and John will have his. No residue is left to share.

The great bulk of cooperative acts do not result from agreement unless the word "agreement" is stretched to breaking point. When I buy a teapot at the price marked on its ticket, it is a bit absurd to declare that this act of social cooperation was the result of a previous agreement between the shopkeeper and all potential aspirants to new teapots. Opportunities for cooperation are mostly generated by the spontaneous competition of market participants and are not the result of negotiated agreement. The participants must adhere to the conventions of just conduct which do not involve agreement between them or anybody else, and that is all.

To be sure, there is a great variety of cooperative acts and relations that are one-off, unique, and not impersonal. Their terms do not emerge from market competition and must be negotiated. If agreement is needed to generate morals, and morals constrain the terms agreements can justifiably have, it is to such negotiated agreements that the argument may possibly be relevant. However, even here fundamental objections stand in the way.

A crucial point in Gauthier's scheme of the agreed moral order is that negotiations must result in the equal sharing of the cooperative gain (presumably, the excess of the Pareto-optimal gain over the gain yielded by a preceding practice). No argument is advanced why we should believe in this far from self-evident requirement. However, the real obstacle is not that this is not self-evident, but that it lacks any ascertainable or even just definable meaning. Gauthier uses "utility" as the entity that, if it existed, would be maximized by a rational individual's revealed and logically well-ordered preferences. How, for pity's sake, can he tell that Will's gain of Will-utility was greater, equal, or smaller than John's gain of John-utility from their cooperative enterprise of crossing the river? As we had learned, to the great dam of classical welfare theory, neither Will, nor John, nor the Impartial Observer can answer such questions without protesting that of course he is merely expressing his strictly personal view of the social welfare function or his value judgment (of which there may be as many different versions as there are persons). Any sharing of the utility gain, assuming there is any technology telling us how the shares can be varied, from Will getting what may seem to you most of the gain to John getting most of it, could be argued to be equal sharing. Any sharing could be said to conform to morals by agreement, or none could. The best escape from this impasse without getting into further and ever more complicated problems would seem to me to abandon the idea of morals originating in agreements or contracts. Doing that would, in addition, also help to dissipate the risk of confusion between contract and contractarianism in the latter of which the contract is redundant.

CONTRACTS OF EXCHANGE AND THE SOCIAL CONTRACT

Some voluntary, self-imposed constrains upon choice are unilateral. The vow or unrequited promise is the most stringent. Hume recognizes "the performance of promises" as one of the key conventions of the social order. Arguably, it is self-referential: compliance with this convention ensures the performance of promises, and promising to comply with any convention transforms that convention into a binding commitment. The possibility of cooperative strategies becoming binding commitments might open a new perspective to social theory, albeit a hypothetical one.

Beyond unilateral agreement lies the contract. It is a pair of voluntarily assumed obligations, each to be discharged by one party in favor of the other. The contract is thus designed to bring about an exchange of performances. Each party would most prefer to receive the performance of the other while escaping his own obligations to perform. However, he would rather perform his obligation than not receive the other party's performance. The contract may provide for simultaneous performance of the obligations of the two parties (such as a "spot" transaction of cash against delivery) or a continuous flow of performances by both parties (such as employment of labor against pay). Such contracts are self-enforcing and in strict logic redundant, except perhaps for the need to define side conditions. The contract comes into its own when the performances to which the parties obliged themselves are to be nonsimultaneous (such as all credit transactions). The enforcement dependence of such contracts may be resolved in a variety of ways. One is the "shadow of the future"; like any iterated prisoners' dilemma, the payoff of each round of a repeated "game" is skewed in favor of due performance because of the forgone gain from future rounds of the game in case default would cause counterparties to cancel future rounds. Performance may additionally be ensured by the force of the convention of promise-keeping. Finally, performance may be entrusted to a specialized agency such as the state. Instead of being entrusted to, it could be appropriated by such an agency which would ordinarily seek to assure for itself the monopoly of exercising this function.

It must not be forgotten that contrary to the underlying postulate of contractarianism, in reality no state has ever been formed at the unanimous wish of its prospective subjects. The origin of states has always been the assumption of power over the prospective governed by the prospective governors, usually by foreign conquerors, with support by a part of the governed purchased with the resources transferred to them from the rest of the governed. It is this standard mechanism that social contract theory seeks to represent in the metaphor of a voluntary contract of exchange between governors and governed.

What nonsimultaneity is to the general contract of exchange, nonunanimity is to the special one of the social contract. Collective choices binding everyone may well not be Pareto-improvements, better for some and worse for none. The most vital ones, dealing with the distribution of goods and bads, are typically conflictual, Pareto-noncomparable. The prospective losers would oppose them, and lest they should veto the choice, the state might coerce them by the threat of violence or other means of pressure, and secure their acquiescence. Social contract theory would typically represent this as a metaphorical contract of exchange where the governed assume obligation of submission or political obedience to collective choices made in defined form or rules, while the governors accept the obligation to make collective choices by these rules and not to resort to violence as long as the rules are obeyed. The collective choice rule, which in modern states tends to be a rule of rule making, may be quite elementary, e.g., "the king (or dictator) has discretion to make all the rules," or highly complex, e.g., voluminous constitutions drafted by committees. Most of these rules restrict, in a great variety of ways, the freedom of collective choices to range over the entire feasible choice set, reserving certain alternatives for individuals to select for themselves. For instance, so-called civil liberties are often held immune from encroachment. Significantly, however, no constitution, past or present, known to me limits the extent to which collective choice may preempt the national product and devote it to public expenditure. Thus, collective choice is tacitly given first call by taxation on society's current product, with the residue left over for individuals to dispose of. The share absorbed by public consumption and public investment is not limited by the choice rule, but by such extra-constitutional contingencies as the resistance of society to taxation and the ability of government to preempt resources from future generations of individuals by increased borrowing.

Social contract theories may imply, if not argue explicitly, that individuals in fact prefer resources to be used for collectively decided purposes which give them greater "utility" than individually acquired goods and services could procure. Collective choice and the public use of resources, then, are a more efficient producer of "utility" than individually chosen use of the same resources would be. As there is no independent way of comparing the marginal utility of public expenditure with the marginal utility his own expenditure procures for each individual (nor with that of the randomly selected representative individual), we must take it that public expenditure produces more because it is chosen. This, of course, justifies the primacy of collective over individual command of resources by a tautology; public is superior to private, for otherwise it would not be chosen. However, if this were true for every comparison between the utility of each and every individual from individual and from collective use of resources, collective choice would be unanimously preferred. It would be Pareto-better; as in contractarianism, all individuals would choose to do what they wished to do; all would opt for the Pareto-superior state over the stateless anarchy that has no collective choice mechanism. There would be no need for a social contract.

Putting this the other way round, social contract theory is saved from redundancy because collective choice is typically Pareto-noncomparable. Some people feel better if there are more public goods, but other people would rather pay less tax or have a smaller national debt weigh upon the future of their children. The social contract, if it existed, would uniformly oblige everybody to submit to the collective choice rule because the rule applies uniformly if it applies at all; no one can choose to exempt himself from it. Everybody accepts the principle of submission. The contract commits all to obey choices made by way of the choice rule whether they like the chosen alternative or not. There is unanimity that nonunanimous collective choices made in previously agreed ways bind everybody.

This is not nice and tender like contractarianism, but closer to resembling actual societies.

Needless to say, nobody is seriously suggesting that a social contract has really been entered into by our forefathers or that if it has it would bind our own generation. The suggestion instead is that starting from a state of nature, rational individuals would willingly enter into such a contract. Moreover, the present state of affairs is one that would have been produced by such a contract. The upshot of the two theses is that the hypothetical social contract lends the state the same legitimacy as a real one would have done.

Hume taught that man does not create and approve of the authority of the state, but acquiesces in it. However, acquiescence comes in many moods: it may be serene or bored, but also bitter and despairing. Social contract theory, if it has any use or effect at all, may have some impact on the mood of acquiescence. The stripped-down hearsay version of it that trickles down from the academic journals to the media and the schoolroom tells the ordinary man that the political and social state of affairs under the authority of government that he passively accepts and often resents, is one that he and his fellows would rationally have chosen. Religion, it has been asserted, is the opium of the people. Should not someone announce now that social contract theory is its Valium?

REFERENCES

Buchanan, J. M. (1975), *The Limits of Liberty: Between Anarchy and Leviathan,* Chicago: University of Chicago Press.

Fudenberg, D., and E. Maskin (1986), "The Folk Theorem in Repeated Games with Discounting or with Incomplete Information," *Econometrica* 54, 533–56.

Gauthier, D. (1986), *Morals by Agreement,* Oxford: Oxford University Press.

Hobbes, T. (1968 [1651]), *Leviathan,* ed. by C. B. MacPherson, New York: Penguin.

Hume, D. (1978), *A Treatise of Human Nature,* reprinted from original edition by L. A. Selby-Bigge, 2nd ed. with text revised and notes by P. H. Nidditch, Oxford: Oxford University Press.

Lewis, D. (1969), *Conventions: A Philosophical Study,* Cambridge, Mass.: Harvard University Press.

Nozick, R. (1974), *Anarchy, State, and Utopia,* New York: Basic Books.

Rawls, J. (1971), *A Theory of Justice,* Cambridge, Mass.: Harvard University Press.

2. ORDERED ANARCHY AND CONTRACTARIANISM

AGREEMENTS AND CONVENTIONS

Sugden reminds us that for Hume (1978), a convention is an agreement of sorts and since agreement and contract are cognate, "it should not be surprising that someone who finds Hume's analysis attractive is also attracted to social contract theory, or vice versa."[1] The two are not in conceptual conflict.

There are, of course, several sorts of agreements. If I meet a friendly stranger and he tells me that it is a lovely day, I will agree that it is indeed lovely. The agreement commits to nothing and stirs to no action. Let it be called Agreement 0. If I see all drivers driving on the right, I conjecture that they find such coordination a good thing and I agree with them, so much so that I, too, will do as they do. My agreement stirs me to emulation. But it is not an agreement *with* them. Call this Agreement 1. The corresponding convention yields mutual advantage, but that is no part of the reason why I adhere to it. The reason is my own advantage. If I did not recognize it and deviated from the convention, most others would still adhere to it. Under Agreement 2, I conjecture that all my neighbors would find it a good thing if their neighbors stole less, or not at all, from them, and they would rather steal less frequently, or indeed not at all, if the neighbors responded to such restraint by like restraint. I agree, and will join them in the corresponding convention by stealing less often or (if the most efficient of the alternative equilibria gets selected) not at all. Note that Agreement 2 is confined to a recognition of identical interests and an identity of responses to be expected from one another. The agreement does

From *Philosophy* 85, 3 (July 2010): 399–403. Reprinted with permission of Cambridge University Press; permission conveyed through Copyright Clearance Center, Inc.

1. Robert Sugden, "Can a Humean Be a Contractarian?" in M. Baurmann and Bernd Lahno (eds.), *Perspectives in Moral Science* (Frankfurt: Frankfurt School Verlag, 2009), 18.

not entail a binding undertaking to perform an action or forbear from one. Mutual advantage results from the convention, but that is not the reason why I adhere to it. It is not an exchange of performances, or of undertakings to exchange performances in the future, though it may look *as if* it were one. Finally, in Agreement 3, which serves as the keystone of the Humean edifice, we all agree to keep our promises. This is an undertaking that reacts upon itself to make it binding, and to render binding all other explicit undertakings. Agreement 3 has two variants, the unilateral or unrequired promise and the reciprocal promise or contract. Hume pays little attention to the former. The latter, rendering exchanges of nonsimultaneous performances feasible, expands the scope for generating mutual advantage beyond the constraint of the cash-on-the-barrelhead type and is a gift of incalculable value to civilization.

By establishing the binding undertaking, Agreement 3 lays what looks like a footbridge leading from noncooperative to cooperative game theory, and also to social contract theory. This terminates the crescendo of agreements.

SOCIAL CONTRACT, OR THE AGREEMENT TO SUBMIT

For all that conventions, contracts, and the social contract are all agreements and linguistically cognate, there are gaps of discontinuity between them and a chasm of unfathomable depth between contract and social contract.

Linguistic cognateness is no excuse for ignoring the incompatibility in what two closely related terms signify. In convention, including its most stringent form, the contract, individual choice prevails throughout. The social contract, on the contrary, is a hypothetical agreement by all members of a society (the "all" invoking an idealized unanimity, to be treated with Wicksellian tolerance) to adopt a meta-rule, a rule of rule-making or constitution, by which nonunanimous decisions can be reached that are binding for all. The social contract legitimizes collective choices to which all individuals have committed themselves to submit.

The social contract differs in its outward form according to who, in the long line of its authors from Aquinas to Rawls, is providing the text.

In Hobbes, the contracting parties create Leviathan, who enforces their covenant with the sword. In Locke, they deal with a sovereign in place who agrees to do certain things and not to do certain others; his subjects agree to obey him as long as he keeps his side of the bargain and may revolt if he does not. In Rousseau, all agree to conform to a General Will that is not necessarily or even probably a will of their own. In Rawls, a duty of fairness persuades all to purge their minds of all that might otherwise induce them to disagree about how the "background institutions" should distribute the basic good things of life. Since they contrive to ignore all relevant differences between them, their social contract is an agreement of one standardized person with himself. In Nozick, all entrust their quarrels and powers to protective agencies that are destined to merge and form the state.

Real-world social contracts in our time, embedded in constitutions, all provide for rule making by nonunanimous vote, the result passing for collective choice entitled to preempt or override individual choice. Individuals accept this *principle of submissions.* They do so in the putative interest they have in the common good (maximization of "the" social welfare function or other words to a similar effect) that collective choice pursues.

ALTERNATIVE REDUNDANCIES

For disciples of Hume, collective choice should be anathema for two major and some minor reasons. One major reason is that the idea of individuals all agreeing to surrender their autonomy and to endow government with power to impose collective choice—instead of the Humean idea of acquiescing in the government that, by "long possession, present possession, or conquest"[2] is already in place—goes right against the Humean grain. The other major reason takes a little longer to state. Hume's great trinity of spontaneous conventions, "the stability of possession, its translation by consent and the performance of promises"[3] satisfy the enabling condition for society to exist. Each

2. David Hume, *A Treatise of Human Nature* (Oxford: Clarendon Press, 1978), 559.

3. *Ibid.*, 541.

convention is brought forth by an equilibrium selection mechanism, a "game" whose solution is payoff-enhancing, advantageous to the "players." In some of these game-like interactions, a free-rider option is a temptation to deviate from the equilibrium. Since ascertainable historical and empirical facts testify to the survival of such conventions, there must be enough "players" using contingent retaliatory strategies to spoil the free-rider payoff and keep deviation in check. The mechanism of generating advantageous coordination equilibria that are self-enforcing thanks to their incentive structure or to retaliation that deters free riders, calls forth not only the great Humean trinity of ownership, transfer, and promise, but a much larger set of greater or smaller conventions that can generate mutual advantage. The set protects against torts, discourages nuisances, and scolds incivilities. Such a set of conventions is the foundational institution of ordered anarchy. In a closed society, this set of conventions suffices to keep the peace and to uphold the social order, and makes the Hobbesian government redundant, just as the creation of such government by social contract makes the set of conventions redundant. Humeans would have no hesitation in deciding which of the two is redundant.

THE CONTRACTARIAN EVASION

Objectors to this condemnation of government usually refer to the small group–large group problem. (Hayek, for one, does so, perhaps making too much of it. Large groups, except crowds, are usually agglomerations of small groups.) Hume was perfectly aware of the small group–large group problem. He nevertheless judged that a society ruled only by its conventions could function as an ordered anarchy if left alone. He declared unambiguously that ". . . I assert the first rudiments of government to arise from quarrels, not among men of the same society, but among those of different societies."[4]

Interestingly, this squares with the experience of modern-day philosophical anarchists whose main difficulty seems to be in showing how a society without government could provide for its own defense against foreign aggression.

4. *Ibid.*, 539–40.

Can Humean social theory make the social contract redundant yet be compatible with it? Sugden evades the obvious fault of trying to have it both ways by separating social contract theory proper (incompatible) from contractarianism (compatible). The separation, if genuine, saves his thesis, but inspection easily reveals that the separation proves impossible where it would really matter.

Briefly, for Sugden contractarianism is the social theory of James Buchanan. It is defined mainly by what it is not: it is not a social contract with the object of pursuing the common good, maximizing some conception of welfare, and ensuring the supply of public goods. On these professed negatives, it does look separate from the standard understanding of the social contract. In contractarianism, we are told, "the role of government is to implement voluntary exchanges."[5] Presumably, exchanges are "implemented" by the parties to the exchange. Does Sugden mean that the role of government is to exchange, or is it to facilitate exchanges by individuals? Be that as it may, no protestations of self-restraint and modesty of ambition alter the fact that contractarianism, like the other social contracts, entails agreement on a constitution permitting the making of rule-bound social choices to which the contracting parties agree to submit. By applying the collective choice rule, one part of society can preempt individual choices in order, among other things to extract resources from the other part. No constitution known to man fails to do so. It would deny its own raison d'etre if it did fail. The redistributive function is consistent with the principle of submission at the heart of any social contract, and it has enough merit to attract some bona fide defenders. Buchanan himself asserts that even those whose resources are habitually extracted approve of this being done, for their own future is shrouded in the "veil of uncertainty" and they might well expect redistribution to work in their favor one day. (One wonders what an insurance underwriter would make of this argument.) In any event, the contractarian constitution not only "implements voluntary exchanges," but keeps engendering collective choices that progressively reduce the scope of these voluntary exchanges relative to the mandatory ones the choice mechanism is geared to multiply.

5. Sugden, 11.

Imputing to individuals a rationally calculated consent to a constitution—any constitution—that must produce this result and has in modern history invariably produced it is inseparable from the contractarian hypothesis. Maybe people do rationally and near-unanimously seek such an outcome; one cannot conclusively deny it. But we should not be asked to believe, as Sugden asks us to do, that contractarianism is something apart from social contract theory and is immune from the latter's vices, so much so that one can without intellectual embarrassment be both a Humean and a contractarian.

REFERENCES

Hume, D. 1978. *A Treatise of Human Nature.* Oxford: Clarendon Press.

Sugden, R. 2009. "Can a Human Being Be a Contractarian?" in M. Baurmann and Bernd Lahn (ed.), *Perspectives in Moral Science.* Frankfurt: Frankfurt School Verlag.

3. INSPECTING THE FOUNDATIONS OF LIBERALISM

THE EMERGENCE OF FIRST PRINCIPLES

The Roots of Justice

As luck would have it, the more important is a concept for the critical understanding of a state of affairs, the more it tends to be clouded from clear view by turgid rhetoric and confused ideas. However, blowing off the fog of verbiage that surrounds a major concept makes the task of clarifying the next one and the one after that progressively easier. As one must begin somewhere, I propose to begin with justice.

Men typically have moral intuitions about what is just and inclinations to accept certain types of acts and facts as admissible while excluding others as inadmissible. Yet neither intuitions nor inclinations make justice. It may be, on the contrary, that they are made by it.

In selecting a course of action, a pattern of behavior, or a strategy of best responses to alternative strategies adopted by others, men must be guided by effective interdictions and commands that tell them what they *must not* do or, less frequently, *must* do. Between them, these effectively enforced restrictions leave a residual of acts, normally far vaster than the specifically enumerated *must nots* and *musts,* that men *may* do. The latter, of course, constitutes the area of de facto liberty. The concept of justice must do no less than explain where these restrictions come from and what purpose they serve. The answers should reveal in what sense they are just.

The restrictions may be deliberately *made,* or they may spontaneously *arise.* For no more profound a reason than easy reference, I shall call the former *laws,* the latter *rules.*

Law is deliberately made by the lawgiver, the judge who decides a case and creates a precedent, the judge who follows the precedent set

From *Economic Affairs* 30, 1 (March 2010): 6–12. Reprinted with permission of John Wiley and Sons; permission conveyed through Copyright Clearance Center, Inc.

by an earlier judge, the legislators who vote a law, the king who decrees one, or the high priesthood that interprets divine revelation. Each and every one of these lawgivers is invested with authority to give it. But where does that authority come from? It could be derived from a higher and stronger authority, but then the same question would present itself with regard to *that* authority or any other yet higher one that one cares to imagine. Alternatively, the authority may be generated by itself in a sort of Indian rope trick, a hypothesis that is not as persuasive as one might require. Finally, the lawgiver might derive the necessary authority from the once-and-for-all, or continually renewed, mandate of all who shall fall under the law to be given. This is the standard solution proffered by political theory, the social contract. Though appealing in its facile rhetoric, this hypothesis has been severely if not mortally wounded by criticism that denies the possible validity or indeed the meaning of a hypothetical unanimous contract among hypothetical persons in a hypothetical situation. Real-life democracy, where a majority implicitly approves the prevailing laws, is not a very good substitute, if only because laws not, or not necessarily, approved by a minority fall short of what justice would demand of a system whose authority is supposed to derive from consensual agreement.

In contrast to *made* law whose legitimacy is ultimately hypothetical, vulnerable to logic, and unable to be confirmed, rules that arise spontaneously have the great strength of being immune to problems of legitimacy. Rules are conventions generally adhered to by a population no member of which can rationally wish that other members should not adhere to it (which need not be the case for given law; in a civil disobedience or taxpayer strike, strikers would wish others to strike, too).

Each convention is an equilibrium solution of a "game" of coordinated behavior in which each player chooses a behavior that will be best for him if other players choose the behavior that will be best for them. Mutual adjustment takes place by trial and error.

Consider a schematic account of how such a rule may emerge. Two clans live incommunicado at opposite ends of a wilderness which members of both frequent to find game or mushrooms. On meeting by chance, each can try to kill the other so as to eliminate competition for game, or give the other a wide berth, or approach with palm upward and smiling reassuringly. The first two choices produce inferior, miserable sorts of equilibria. To reach the third, the first mover takes the risk that the second mover will not appreciate his smile and will kill him. However, if things pass as the first mover has expected, the word may spread and more people will risk the peaceful approach than take a one-in-two chance of getting killed anyway in each hostile encounter. Reliance on encounters passing off peacefully will produce such benefits for the two clans as trade and exogamy. The convention-based rule "do not kill peaceful strangers" will be cemented. It will be in everyone's interest that no one should deviate from it; hence there will be benefits or avoided losses to set against the cost of deterring deviation by punishing the deviants.

A number of complications surround conventions with awkward incentive structures where deviation pays better than compliance once most others comply or where compliance does not pay unless enough others comply. Temptation to free-ride on the unwillingness of others to incur costs to punish deviants—a version of the public goods dilemma—could also be a problem. Nevertheless, whatever the problems that had to be resolved, the overwhelming evidence is that essential conventions have in fact duly arisen and taken root in much the same form in all civilizations. They have mostly survived the competition of government-made law which has widely resorted to adapting and using them as the foundation of more elaborate (and, as the present author would claim, less legitimate and often less impartial and less just) legal superstructures. These conventions have the rank of universal rules of behavior. Unlike natural law or morality, they are ascertainable facts of history and anthropology; we can tell where they come from and why they have the form they do.

Rules of behavior are above all anti-tort rules. They protect person, property, peaceful pursuits, and the binding nature of reciprocal promises (contracts). They do these things by prohibitions interdicting serious bodily harm and the use or threat of violence except in defense of these rules, theft, robbery, fraud, usurpation, and default on obligations. They protect peaceful pursuits by virtue of prohibiting behavior that would significantly interfere with another's peaceful pursuits. Thus, while there is no rule affirming the freedom of speech, acts that would interfere with it—gagging, intimidation, forcible denial of the commercial freedom to buy newsprint or wavelength—would be barred by the rules.

Less vital and less universal rules are aimed at nuisances and incivilities. Pollution and loutish behavior have become major complaints comparatively recently, well after it became the standard expectation that it is the state's task to deal with all ills, an expectation encouraged by the state itself. Hence the spontaneous rise of conventions against nuisances and incivilities was less vigorous than of those dealing with personal integrity, property, and contract that date back to an age of less pervasive state action. If this proves anything, it is the effectiveness of the state's affirmation of its monopoly of law-making and police powers.

I will call the system of coordinated behavior made up entirely of conventionally based rules a *situation of perfect justice.* It is perfect at least in the sense that all its rules are voluntarily assumed. None is imposed by authority that would have to depend on some justification that may itself be contestable, other than being self-evidently uncontestable.

Freedom and Its Presumption

Occasionally, attempts have been made to read different meanings into the two words "liberty" and "freedom." I think this is a mistake liable to lead to confusion. I will treat them as synonyms and use one or the other as chance might dictate.

A corollary of the principle of perfect justice characterized in the preceding section is the *principle of perfect freedom.* Perfect justice defines the acts that none must do to another's person or his belongings, such acts counting as *wrongs.* Perfect freedom by implication defines the set of all acts that are free, not wrongs as they violate no conventional rules and are free precisely by virtue of certain other acts being wrongs, i.e., rule violations.

A palpable way of seeing this is to regard the rules of perfect justice as a fence that excludes wrongs, with every act one can perform while staying inside the fence being a liberty. The fact that the fence is ascertainable, testified to by anthropology, history, and the evidence of our everyday experiences, is of fundamental importance to political theory. It can act as the coveted Archimedean fixed point, an absolute reference to which the moves of a movable world can be related.

The justice and liberty expressed by the rule system are "perfect" in much the same sense as the "perfect competition" of economics is perfect. The latter is a heuristic device, not meant to represent a real state of affairs, but to help to understand its polar opposite, monopoly and the real-world zone in-between that Roy Harrod baptized imperfect competition. Real-world justice and by the same token real-world freedom are imperfect. Upon their pristine state is superimposed a structure of laws that are intrinsically unjust and constitute an encroachment on the fenced-in area that, under perfect freedom, would be the exclusive reserve of free acts.

These laws are products of collective choice and are unjust in the sense that all collective choice is unjust because it is the imposition of a choice by some on others. The choice may be made by a dictator and his tacit or overt supporters, or by bare majority vote, or any other source of decision intermediate between the two, and is imposed by its authority and power on those who, but for the imposition, might not have made the same choice. The nature of collective choice is unjust in that it overrides individual choice without its de facto ability to do so being property justified, i.e., rooted in justice itself.

It may be pertinently objected that when collective choice coerces the individual to abandon its preferred choice, it is doing no more than is done to adherents to a convention, e.g., the convention not to steal, when they punish the thief, redress the tort he committed, and force him, by the threat of rule enforcement, to comply with the rule. He would prefer to go on stealing, but his preference is being overridden. However, the analogy is not a genuine one. Collective choice imposes the preference of some on others without any prejudice to the justice or otherwise of the one or the others. We might properly call this first-order coercion. By contrast, enforcement of a rule of justice imposes compliance and deters a deviant individual choice springing from an unjust preference. We can legitimately distinguish this imposition from collective choice in general by calling it second-order.

At this juncture, it seems to me urgent to examine—to reduce their flow to a trickle would be much too much to hope—two sources of confusion that have poisoned a great deal of liberal thinking. They are associated with the names of two reputedly liberal theorists, J. S. Mill and John Rawls.

Mill's famous Harm Principle is thought to lay down that preventing harm to others is an adequate ground for suppressing acts causing such harm. Fairness to Mill demands that we read him strictly, and on a strict reading he takes harm to others to be a necessary reason for coercion, but not a sufficient one. As it is, however, he is widely held to be granting a liberal *nihil obstat* to acts preventing harm. Harm, however, is an open-ended holdall, a thoroughly mushy concept that fits almost any conceivable act. Giving alms to a beggar harms the other beggar who suffers from greater need. It must be prohibited and the money of alms givers centrally administered so as to prevent the most harm. Any frivolous claim about being harmed by, say, competition in trade or an elitist educational practice has a putative liberal argument in its favor under the broad reading of the Harm Principle.

Equally insidious, if not more so, is John Rawls's First Principle of Justice, by which everybody must have a *right* to the greatest possible liberty compatible with the same liberty for all. One is struck by the glaring redundancy of the word *right,* for what he presumably meant to say was that everybody must have the greatest possible liberty compatible with the same for all. If the definitional analysis at the start of this section is logically acceptable, liberty is the sum of acts that do not violate rules, i.e., are not wrong and hence must not be wronged by acts that violate rules.

To say with Rawls that one has a right to liberty is tantamount to saying that one has a right not to be wronged—a fatuous statement. Why does one need a "right" to do what is not prohibited? The liberty of an act *means* that an actor is at liberty to carry out the act and it is hard to comprehend what the word "right" is doing here unless—a hugely important "unless"—liberty is not the logical corollary of rule compliance so that no objection arises against the doing of it, but a *privilege* one does not have unless endowed with a specific *right* to it. Free speech, then, does not mean that you can speak your mind. It means that you can speak your mind if you have the right to do so. The right, in turn, must have been granted by some person or entity entitled to grant it. Such an idea is not merely strange but also repugnant and merits no further scrutiny.

It may of course well be that Rawls did not think through the avalanche of nonsensical or downright malignant implications of his use of the term "right." He may just have fallen in, without conscious intent, with the fashion of his day that made "right" and "rights-based" the obligatory buzzwords in any political theory aspiring to modernity. The consequences of the onset of "rightsism" have been far-reaching. Not only have a number of liberties underlying the normal course of public affairs been made dependent on "civil rights," but a multitude of wholly original "rights" have been injected into the political consciousness of governors and governed. Mindful of the manifold desiderata and niceties that add up to well-being, political theorists have generously distributed rights to adequate nourishment, proper shelter, education, "cultural development," and employment compatible with human dignity. No notice was taken of the fact that these putative rights had no practical effect beyond raising false expectations if the corresponding obligations to provide food, shelter, education, and employment were not imposed on those able to provide them, nor of the possibility that imposing them might be to wrong some or all of the involuntary obligors. Woolly thinking has landed "rightsism" in the same redistributive maze as the utilitarianism which it condemned and sought, reasonably enough, to replace.

Wittgenstein said that it was certain that he was more than three years old. There are some similar certitudes about free and unfree acts. Reading a page of this essay is clearly free, torturing a child is clearly not free. However, there is a vast array of acts, including their possible but uncertain ramifications, where the case is not obviously one or the other. Opinions differ; the proposer affirms that the act is free and must not be hindered, the opponent contends that it is not free and should be prohibited. Is there a general rule for resolving such a question?

If we say that we must take *X* to be the case unless non-*X* is proved, there is a presumption in favor of *X* and the burden of proof to the contrary lies with non-*X*. There is a general presumption of freedom if an act is allowed to pass unless sufficient reason is shown why it should be prohibited. But why should the presumption be in favor of permission instead of prohibition? The answer is provided by the asymmetry between two forms of validating a statement, namely verification and falsification. If the burden of proof were placed on the proposer of an act, he would have to show that every potential objection to his proposed act was false, i.e., that there is no sufficient reason against it. If possible objections were numerous, falsifying them all would be very costly. If they were infinitely many, falsification would be impossible. Knowing what he was objecting to, on the other hand, the objector could at least attempt to verify that he has sufficient reason for objecting; his attempt need not be costly and it is logically not impossible. Verification being at least more feasible than falsification, the burden of proof falls on the opponent of an act and there is a presumption of freedom. To take the opposite position would be to deal, not with a needle in the haystack, but with a wisp of hay in a needlestack. Every act would be prohibited unless sufficient reason was shown why it should be permitted.

In a world where everybody's every possible act was prohibited unless sufficient reason was shown that it should be allowed either because the act was such or the person wishing to carry it out was such that the prohibition ought to be lifted, there would be a presumption of unfreedom. The burden of proof would be carried by the proposer. It is he who would have to show that the act in question deserves a licence, or that he should have the privilege (the "right") to perform it. In that world, going about the ordinary business of life would be cumbersome, and enforcing the prohibition of everything unless it was specifically exempted would be very, very costly. Posting blanket licences and "rights" for part of the universe of possible acts in anticipation of particular claims for them would expedite matters. A Bill of Rights that tells you what you may assuredly do is a solemn example of such a posting. It would be comic if it were not so sad and depressing that Bills of Rights, logically a by-product of an underlying presumption of unfreedom, are persistently mistaken for bulwarks of liberty.

Property and Capitalism

It is easy intuitively to grasp why conventions for the protection of property and contract would spontaneously emerge as coordination equilibria of "games" where respect for another's property and contractual rights was the best response to his respect for yours. For Hume, there were three conventions that jointly constituted and secured property: "the stability of possession," "its translation by consent," and "the keeping of promises." (Had he said "reciprocal promises," i.e., contracts, the matter would have been even clearer, for unilateral promises that do not constitute contracts would have been excluded.) It is these conventions that he regarded as basic preconditions of a society and "antecedent to the state."

It is less evident, and not explicitly laid down by Hume, how a resource becomes someone's property to begin with. He did not deem it necessary to demolish, or indeed to pay much attention to, Locke's treatment of this crucial starting point that has since cast doubt on the legitimacy of property and forced some liberal thinkers to seek utilitarian and other excuses for it—excuses that tacitly grant some validity to Locke's strange argument.

Locke takes it that nothing is really unowned in the first place, for God has given everything to mankind. Appropriating a resource is taking it out of mankind's joint tenancy for the exclusive use of the first individual acquirer. He incurs a debt to mankind that he redeems by satisfying Locke's Second Proviso, that is, by "leaving enough and as good for others." The proviso is void if God has not given everything to mankind, a belief one is not morally or otherwise obliged to hold. It has lastingly muddled the issue by suggesting its legitimacy to a proviso that cannot ever be satisfied except by a fluke and that has never in fact been satisfied.

The "fluke" case is one where the world's valuable resources are of uniform mass and are divided into a number of equal parts, this number being larger than the number of people in the world aspiring to be first acquirers. Each aspirant is allowed one part. After the last aspirant has taken his part, there is still "enough and as good" left over. If there is no leftover, the last aspirant has failed to satisfy the Lockean proviso; his acquisition is illegitimate. By backward induction, so is that of the last-but-one acquirer, as is that of the last-but-two, and so on to the first. Except in the "fluke" case, no first acquisition could be legitimate. However, since among normally motivated aspirants the process of first acquisition would be unlikely to end with a leftover, the "fluke" case can perhaps safely be dismissed as no more than a scholastic exercise of the imagination.

In the real world, the supply of unowned resources looks like being relatively inelastic. Except for the occasional lucky strike, additional resources can only be found at increasing finding costs in terms of exploration and research. "Enough and as good" is not left over to successive acquirers because they must generally incur successively higher finding costs.

In sum, if the world is owned collectively by mankind, as Locke would have it, his own proviso effectively excludes legitimate ownership by individuals. If his proviso is ignored, as I believe it must be on the grounds set out above, scope opens for property to emerge as a conventional solution of an obvious game-like interaction between a potential owner of a resource and the other nonowners who, expecting analogous interactions to occur again and again, will find it to their best advantage to acquiesce in the ownership of the former. Repetition of the interaction offers each a chance at Buggins's[1] turn, with reciprocity becoming the equilibrium strategy.

A convention that first acquisition of a resource confers good title on the acquirer, qualifying it as his property, can be traced back to two logically prior conventions. One is "first come, first served," which concedes ownership of a known resource to whomever first takes possession of it. The solution of the game could never be "first come, second served" because then everybody would refuse to arrive first and no one would arrive at all. The other fundamental convention is "finders keepers," that confers ownership of a hitherto unknown resource to whomever discovers it. Underground and subsea exploration and inventing, giving rise to intellectual property, should logically fall under this convention, though in practice they do so only within limits, as subsurface finds partly accrue to the royalty owner and the state, while patent rights have a limited life span.

The legitimacy and self-enforcing stability of property, a first principle of liberalism, may be understood as an edifice of spontaneous conventions. At its base, "first come, first served" and "finders, keepers" justify first acquisition. Rising therefrom, "Buggins's Turn" explains its tolerance by others. Topping them, the Humean conventions of "possession, transference and promises" assures the functions of ownership.

Opposed to this system of conventional rules is the radically different conceptual schema of "property rights." The liberal principle of ownership is neither derived from nor enforced by any authority. Its

1. Idiom calls Buggins all men who get their turn without regard to their deserts or powers.

content is a set of liberties the owner may employ, notably the liberty of use, usufruct, contract, and disposition. Property "rights," by contrast, must be conferred upon the right holder by some higher authority, most plausibly by the state, which normally also takes responsibility for their protection against all, though not against itself. In an earlier section we have discussed the insidious effects of confusing rights and liberties, talking of rights when liberties are meant, and invoking "rights to liberties." There is no need to rehearse the same argument here. (It may be worth mentioning, however, that the caveat about "rights" does not apply to the other, and genuine, sense of property rights. The latter are elements of contracts relating to property; for example, a lender's right to interest and repayment or an option holder's right to exercise the option. Political theory uses the term "property rights" in the other, confused and insidious sense.)

Do liberalism and capitalism mean the same thing? Though the answer, namely "no," requires little hesitation or reflection, there is a great deal of overlap between the two. Despite Engels's somewhat clumsy effort to identify a "state capitalism" as distinct from socialism, capitalism cannot sensibly be dissociated from the ownership of capital being ultimately vested in individuals, even if corporate owners, such as pension funds and other intermediaries, are interposed. A large part of the freedoms ring-fenced by the conventional rules of justice, such as consumer choice and more generally the freedom of contract, are closely associated with capitalism and may be necessary conditions of any rigorous conception of it. Yet in everyday speech an economy could reasonably be called capitalist even if its legislation restricted such liberties as that of religion, assembly, or the press. Nor would the least infringement by the state of the freedom of contract by way of tariffs, quotas, regulations, subventions, and licences have to prevent us from regarding an economic system as capitalist. However, the infringement of the freedom of contract, whether in the name of the public interest or as part of corporatist practices, must not fatally weaken the defining feature of capitalism, namely the clear division between the interests of labor and capital. In precapitalist and small-scale production, these two factors are supplied by the same person and the whole value added accrues to him. The artisan owns his tools, the serf or the small farmer his draft animal, the merchant his stock in trade.

Nothing signals the relative productivity of his labor and his capital. Only the undivided total of the two is ascertainable. Something like this indivision is hankered after by socialist thought in which all capital is supposed to be owned by labor. In capitalism, a firm's supply of labor and of capital are provided by two distinct sets of persons. They jointly produce the value added, and each would increase his share of it at the expense of the other. An infinite number of different bargains between the two are possible.

There is only one, though, in which the firm itself is in equilibrium. This is where the risk-adjusted factor rewards are equal to the marginal products of the factors. If the wage rate were lower than this, the firm would gain by hiring more labor, and if it were higher, it would gain by shedding labor. Likewise, if its rate of profit were higher than its cost of capital, it would seek to attract more capital, and vice versa. In a dynamic economy where every variable is liable to change over time, this equilibrium must be conceived in terms of expected values and its analysis runs the danger of becoming somewhat tautological. But in any event, the capitalist firm is as close to being a compass tending to point to allocative efficiency as one can hope to get.

Though it is an intellectually somewhat sordid anticlimax, this section must wind up with a reminder about how these matters appear in English English and American English. This part of the present essay seeks to explicate liberalism as it appears in English English usage. It is not evident what American English would call it; perhaps conservatism or "neoliberalism" (though the "neo" would be a little hard to fit with the theses here proposed). American English would call "liberal" the infringements of the freedom of contract. Above all, it would call "liberal" the particular doctrine and practice that I propose to qualify as the corruption of liberalism and that is the subject of the following section.

THE CORRUPTION OF LIBERALISM

"Liberal Democracy"

The term "liberal democracy" has in recent decades become the standard way to refer to the liberal form of government. The first principles of liberalism are fully compatible only with ordered anarchy, a spontaneously emerging framework of conventional rules. Even imperfectly liberal orders are biased toward small government. Democracy has historically been associated with a dynamic, expansionary area of collective choice, in the shape of big government. Coupling "liberal" and "democracy" could hardly be more incongruous than "smallbig government."

Democracy, where a voting majority or at least plurality is needed for mandating a government to make collective choices that bind all they are aimed at regardless of whether they consent or dissent, may be the limiting case of bigness in government, but in general all forms or rule systems of governing a state are antagonistic to liberalism. Any government, even the firmest dictatorship or the most time-honored absolute monarchy, obtains political obedience by relying on support from its partisans. It buys this support by transferring to them periodic or continuing gifts of privilege, influence, wealth, and income extracted from the rest of society. Whatever form the extraction and the transfer may take, ancient as grants of land and licences to trade, or modern as complex taxation, welfare entitlements, and public goods serving mainly particular groups, it remains the quintessential mechanics for governments to secure sufficient obedience and hence power over the state.

Democracy is credited by conventional wisdom with the ability to permit replacing one government by another without recourse to violence or its threat. However, peaceful transfer of power is owed, not to democracy, but to the rule of law. Whatever law regulates the tenure and transfer of power, it will ensure peaceful transition if it is respected. An intricate choreography of minorities electing other minorities until a government was designated secured for Venice for the best part of a millennium remarkably peaceful political changes without the least move toward a democratic franchise. On the other hand, without the rule of law, the pretence of observing democratic manners of going about the assignment of power have only too often failed to produce its transfer, let alone a peaceful one, as modern African history illustrates.

Nevertheless, the impact of democracy on the liberal order of things differs distinctly from that of any other form of government. Where material interest is a significant element in political motivation, even when it does not dominate it, buying support by taking resources mainly from one part of the voting public and giving it to another is a necessary condition of securing and maintaining power, but how much redistribution is sufficient for the purpose depends on two features of the form of government as defined by rules and tradition. One is the proportion of the social body whose support must be secured. If it is organized and well led within a society that is leaderless and not organized, the proportion may be a small fraction of the total, such as a Praetorian guard or a KGB-style political police. Buying its fidelity takes relatively little redistribution. The other determining feature of how much redistribution may suffice is the degree to which rules and tradition allow political competition. Where overt rivalry for power is an illicit activity, and is suppressed as a matter of course, relatively little redistribution may be required to secure acquiescence in the status quo. Obviously, the opposite is true where competition for voters is at the center of political life and rival contenders for power must each aim at attracting no less than one-half of the total of votes plus one.

On both counts, then, it is democracy, understood simply as a collective choice rule, that attaches the mandate to decide to persons attracting a greater number of anonymous votes than their rivals, with redistribution as a means of maximizing the chance to acquire and hold the power to govern.

It is hardly necessary to spell out the consequence of this for liberalism. Whether by conviction or by dire need, democratic governments are condemned by political competition constantly to press against the frontier that divides individual from collective choices. They must willy-nilly swallow up and regurgitate a part of the resources produced by society, a part large enough to attract a winning coalition in the face of competition by rivals similarly seeking to form a winning coalition.

As the share of total product preempted by collective choice increases, the cost of extracting it and preserving for government the secure tenure of power by enforcing political obedience rises, too, and beyond some point it is likely to rise faster than the increase in resources preempted. This would seem adequately to explain why collective choice is not maximized until it finally absorbs all of the product, but under current conditions in the Western world hovers between two-fifths and three-fifths of it, though historically its trend slopes upward. Other explanations may complement this one without contradicting it. This gives a measure of the reduction of free choice that depends on the use of material resources.

Corrosive Language

One of the most fascinating and also most ominous developments in the political thought of the last hundred years or so is the role of language in masking erosion of the foundations of liberalism and indeed its direct corrosive effect upon them.

The misuse of language in the course of employing it as a tool of persuasion is only rarely a deliberate strategy. More often and more insidiously, it is an inadvertent distortion that helps the speaker reconcile reality that he is willing to accept with the norms and ideals he believes he ought to adhere to. A small book could be filled with flagrant examples of this practice one might call unconsciously clever sloppiness of expression. Such a book ought urgently to be written. Here, space confines me to a single example.

It has become almost obligatory practice to speak of "liberalism with social justice" in the same breath, as if the latter were a possible aspect or complement of the former. In reality, the mechanism of democracy (and with a lesser degree of probability, any competitive political system) has redistribution as its consequence. Redistribution violates one of liberalism's founding first principles, justice, whose roots are almost timeless, spontaneously arising conventions against torts. Masking the violation of justice, and masking an act of necessary political expedience as a response to moral command, current language evolves the term "social" justice. The amazing speed with which the term passes into noncontroversial, commonly accepted usage is truly remarkable. It is remarkable that it is treated as a branch of justice, though it lacks the latter's defining characteristic, namely a system of rules by which just acts are distinguished from unjust acts. Lacking rules, it is impossible ever to decide that a state of affairs *is* socially just and not in need of redress. The logical corollary, of course, is that the requirement of social justice is never satisfied even in an idealized situation where any desired distribution of goods and bads can be completely and instantaneously achieved by the appropriate policy. It is also remarkable because it is both a sort of branch of justice and a sort of super-justice with undisputed power to override justice itself, notably in matters of property and contract. Finally, it is remarkable because it at least implicitly claims for itself a moral ascendancy whose basis is shrouded in fog but in vague outline seems to be some notion of equality. This notion, in an undefined and impressionistic guise, is represented as self-evident and uncontested. However, when specified, only its almost wholly noncommittal varieties turn out to be uncontroversial: nobody disagrees with "equal respect" or with "equal concern" for all fellow humans. But varieties of equality that benefit some while hurting others commit the equalizer to benefiting one side and are not self-evident. Efforts to deduce the moral superiority of egalitarian over inegalitarian distributions from ethical first principles have sometimes been fashionable but never lastingly successful. However, for everyday popular usage it established itself by virtue of the back-and-forth coupling of the two vague and undefined notions: equality was just for it was part of social justice, and social justice was just for it strove for equality. Though this circularity ceases to function in the face of hard questions of actual distribution, it powerfully influences the general political climate.

The Foundations Perdure

Pursuing the architectural metaphor of my title, how do we view today's social edifice? No amount of indulgence can conceal that it is a hodgepodge of styles adding up to no style. Those who assume responsibility for the way it has turned out call it eclectic and pragmatic, believing these words to be words of approval. The building is dysfunctional, wasteful of effort, marred by ill-fitting parts. It incorporates some of the crumbling walls of its precursor, the old liberal superstructure, though many clamor for knocking them down and replacing them with cinder block. Despite its rickety looks, the present edifice stands up, though perhaps only just. It is habitable, though only just.

For the liberal who is aware of being one, but also for the unconscious one who merely thinks that society should function to mutual advantage and its members should never knowingly invite an authority over themselves, an inspection of the foundations of liberalism must be a source of anxiety. Willingly, or at least thoughtlessly and inadvertently, civil society transferred the function of enforcing its rules of coexistence to a specialized agency, or allowed the latter to assume it by usurpation. As a probably unavoidable consequence, the agency asserted the monopoly of the use of force and established a mechanism for both provoking and executing collective choices that could and often did override individual ones and preempt the scope of the latter.

The agency of enforcement, developing into an ever more elaborately organized state, relies not only on its monopoly of physical force, but also on the support of some part of the society it governs. It secures the support it needs for assured tenure and obedience to its orders by buying a winning coalition of supporters with resources extracted from the losing coalition. Thus, redistribution in often complex ways by both taxing and spending is intrinsic in political systems that rely partly or wholly on the consent of the governed.

This is in flagrant violation of justice conceived as spontaneously adopted conventions to secure mutually advantageous behavior. The violation is camouflaged by declaring it to be a requirement of social justice, a kind of justice entitled to supersede the justice proper whose roots are the mutually advantageous conventional equilibria.

The foundations of liberalism, then, are buried under layers of political practice and worn down by the corrosive language that seeks to pass off antiliberal ideas and practices as complementary with modern liberalism.

The wonder of it all is that in the midst of all this ill use and jeopardy, the foundations of liberalism perdure. They continue to dominate the main outlines of the social structure of Western societies and even exert some incipient effect upon Eastern and Southern ones. The basic rule of property is still that what is mine is not thine, and vice versa. Deviations from this rule need to be specially validated. The basic rule of liberty is still that what is feasible is free unless duly prohibited, rather than that everything is prohibited unless you have a specific "right" to perform the act in question. The basic rule of immunity from wrongful harm is still that others are prohibited from doing wrong, rather than that you have a "right" not to be wronged. Misdeeds are not entirely the fault of society or the victim; the perpetrator does bear some responsibility.

The basic rule of exchange is still that price should equate supply with demand rather than provide a "fair return." Despite ceaseless agitation against them, and despite relentless attempts to legislate or regulate them away, these fundamentals of liberalism show a tenacity and longevity that should give liberals a modest measure of confidence in the future of their creed. The social superstructure may be ungainly and confusing in its details, but what is left of its underlying foundation may yet redeem it.

PART 4

Errors and Omissions

1. SUCKERS, PUNTERS, PATHBREAKERS

WHEN *HOMO OECONOMICUS* IS SELFLESSLY SELFISH

Rational choice presupposes that people do what they like better than any available alternative. If, however, we mistrust what they declare to like or what psychology is supposed to tell us about it (a pardonable enough mistrust), we can only infer what they like from observing what they do. We must be content with revealed preference. The theory of choice is locked into the tautology of "they do what they like because they like what they do," and requiring their preferences to be orderly and consistent is of little practical help. In its elegance, modern choice theory, as represented in neoclassical economics, is too smooth and slippery to be very useful.

The resulting frustration seems to me to have two consequences. One is a more or less unconscious backsliding into old-fashioned utility theory. We know more than revealed preference tells us; we know what people like, therefore we can predict their choices (more or less) before knowing what they chose. They like "utility," the motive for choice. More formally, the things a person likes are arguments in his "utility function" that he seeks to maximize if he is rational. Further tempting detours on this road may lead to suppositions about a stable relation between "utility" and income (the "diminishing marginal utility of money") and about the addition and subtraction of different people's "utilities," both suppositions permitting irresistibly attractive conclusions about "maximizing aggregate social utility" and others of the same family.

The second consequence of the apparently barren elegance of modern choice theory is a repudiation of the backsliding involved in the first. The somewhat outdated utility theory of the latter points almost (though not altogether) inevitably to a *homo oeconomicus* who is op-

From *Cato Journal* 31, 2 (2011): 377–87. Reprinted by permission.

portunistic, self-interested, selfish. The lowbrow criticism of this image is that "neoliberal man is only interested in money," while the highbrow one constructs ingenious laboratory experiments to confirm the evidence of everyday life—namely, that he often behaves as if he were not very interested in money. He will at certain junctures appear actually to be sacrificing his self-interest either for no discernible reason or in favor of some ideal, such as some notion of fairness. Of course, revealed preference remains unbeaten by all this. Man does what he does because that is what he likes better than doing anything else at that juncture. Opting for what he wishes is opportunistic and selfish, though it may be that he wishes the fulfillment of the wish of others and, acting accordingly, could only be described as selfless. If, as logic leads us to recognize, all choice is selfish, his conduct should perhaps be classified as "selflessly selfish." This term is droll and impressionistic, but it does help to dispel the crude notion that rational choice means something like "maximizing money income."

However, lest matters should start to look too easy, we must notice some very important junctures where behavior seems to be motivated by selfless selfishness, but where this refinement is in fact unnecessary, for typical choices can be shown to be rational in a simpler sense. Though there may well be others, the most significant of these choices are made by the sucker who contributes to a public good, the punter who makes the risky first move in an equilibrium selection for a "game," and the pathbreaker who pioneers a new way rather than leave it to others to do it.

THE SUCKER FOR PUBLIC GOODS

Conventional wisdom, codified in Mancur Olson's *The Logic of Collective Action*, has it that, as a general rule, rational agents do not voluntarily contribute to the cost of public goods (Olson 1965). In a large number case, each person's contribution to the cost of the public good would be relatively small. Since the benefits of the pure public good flow to everyone, and the cost of exclusion is prohibitive, each person would try to free ride—getting the benefits without contributing to the costs. If everyone acted in this fashion, there would be no voluntary provision of the public good, even though production would yield net social benefits.

The character of *homo oeconomicus* should forbid him to play the sucker and contribute voluntarily. If suckerdom is to be explained, it must be in behavioristic terms: The contribution was made out of solidarity with one's community, by a wish to look honest and not be despised as a free rider, or by decency proper. The sucker chooses the decent thing because he likes it better than available alternatives. However, a fairly plausible argument shows *homo oeconomicus* willingly acting the sucker under far from extravagant assumptions and without his having any care for solidarity, decency, or the semblance.

Let there be a small riverbank town that has had flood damage and seeks to protect itself from future floods. Consultants present the residents of the town with a probability distribution of floods of various severity over the foreseeable future, the corresponding damage, and the cost of the size of dam needed to protect against a flood of a particular severity. The consultants also calculate the ideal size of dam—namely, one whose marginal cost is just equal to the probability-weighted marginal damage that would be caused by the particular size of flood that the town would suffer if it chose to build a smaller and cheaper dam. Whoever is entitled to interpret the town's wishes decodes that an attempt should be made to build this ideal dam, which can be expected to yield a total benefit (avoided damage, virtual benefit) in excess of its total cost. It is this dam that can be expected to maximize its benefit as a public good.

There being no social contract obliging the townspeople to pay the taxes that a collective choice mechanism (e.g., a voting majority) imposes, the mayor calls for volunteers to pledge a contribution toward the dam's cost. If the sum is undersubscribed, the pledges are cancelled as if nothing had happened; if it is oversubscribed, the pledges are reduced pro rata. How the subscription is going is kept secret until it closes.

What does a rational individual do? If he does not subscribe but enough others do, the dam gets built and he, a free rider, benefits from its protection without bearing any of its cost. Conventional wisdom has it that free riding dominates suckerdom. On a closer look and within the assumptions made in this section, however, this is not the case—in effect, there is no dominant strategy.

Ignoring what his fellow townspeople will choose to do (though having fragmentary bits of information about their dispositions), each individual must act as if he faced a probability distribution of the decisions of the others. The distribution ranges from one extreme where no one subscribes to the other extreme where all subscribe. Somewhere in between there is a probability that just enough others subscribe to make his own eventual contribution decisive for the success or failure of the attempt to find voluntary funding for the dam. If the proportion of subscribers is between zero and the decisive one, our rational individual would expect to do better to subscribe. Not subscribing and hoping that the dam will get built anyway would be to gamble against the odds. Subscribing, on the other hand, commits him to nothing in case the subscriptions of the others are insufficient, commits him to subscribe if his subscription is the decisive one, and commits him to a reduced subscription if more than the decisive proportion of the others subscribe. Only in the latter eventuality would he expect to be better off by taking a gamble on free riding, with the dam getting built without any contribution on his part.

Thus, while there is no dominant strategy and the thesis that free riding is dominant in collective action proves to be invalid under assumptions that are less than extravagant, presumptions can be formed about contingent strategies likely to be adopted by rational persons. Such a person will be the more likely to volunteer to be the sucker the smaller is the likely proportion of others doing the same. The converse is true for the likelihood of the rational person opting for the free-rider role.

This conclusion undermines to a significant extent the general belief that the imperative need of a society for public goods justifies submission to the coercive authority of the state, for only by coerced taxation can public goods be provided. The latter belief can be upheld only by conceiving of public goods as wholly or almost wholly divisible, so that each marginal contribution to the cost of such a good increases the benefit it provides to the public by a marginal amount, hence by near-nothing to any single member of the public, such as the contributor. If so, he would contribute only under coercion or some form of altruism or solidarity with others. However, the very concept of a public good—namely, that access to it is neither excluded nor rationed, and that every member of the public consumes it freely at his discretion without depriving any other member of the public from doing the same—entails that the public good is an indivisible whole "tailored" to its purpose and the size of the public for whose unrestricted consumption it is destined. It is more like a dam than a school lunch.

In the language of neoclassical (and also of Austrian) economics, indivisibility dethrones the marginal and enthrones the decisive contribution. Marginal productivity is either zero or equal to total productivity. When total contributions are just sufficient to produce the public good, each contribution is decisive, for its withdrawal would entail failure of publicness of the good. Hence, the marginal product of each contribution is equal to the total product, the indivisible public good. This manner of putting the matter is to squeeze its logic to the point of abusing it. However, it is a useful abuse if it illuminates, albeit from an unusual angle, the strong force that makes people in important contexts act selflessly selfish.

THE PUNTER IN EQUILIBRIUM SELECTION

In noncooperative games with multiple equilibria, it cannot be predicted which of the potential ones will turn out to be the solution of the game. One equilibrium being Pareto-optimal, or at least greatly superior to another, is no reason for expecting it to be selected. The actual choice of one equilibrium can, of course, always be explained by imputing to the players behavioral motives that would appear consistent with, and adequate to provoke, the actual choice. More ambitiously, an ex post explanation in the rational-choice rather than the behavioral mode can also be constructed by imputing to each player appropriate conjectures about the other player. Admittedly, they cannot generate valid predictions. What they can do, though, is to improve our understanding of the problematic nature of equilibrium selection. They may, in particular, help to identify the circumstances under which the selection of mutually more advantageous, Pareto-superior solutions becomes more rather than less likely. Selection of a particular equilibrium out of the potentially available ones may occur ex nihilo or by way of changing over from another, preexisting equilibrium.

In the latter case, the player who seeks to initiate the change must take a gamble whose odds are hidden in the recesses of the other player's mind. The first player, by abandoning the existing equilibrium, loses its protection. He suffers losses, and the other player reaps gains, that continue until either the second player follows the lead of the first and they create a new equilibrium, or the first player gives up his initiative and reverts to the protection of the old equilibrium. Prima facie, he is a hero, like the soldier who volunteers to be the first over the parapet and advances without assurance of being backed up. He does it because, as we may say analytically, he would rather do it than not do it, or he selfishly pleases himself; however, as his course of action is also an attempt to serve his side's interest it may claim to be selflessly selfish. It can be argued, though, and will be argued below, that sheltering behind the parapet of the old equilibrium is not a dominant strategy; that being a punter in the equilibrium selection attempt is perfectly consistent with being a *homo oeconomicus;* and that selflessness may (but by no means need) mean self-sacrifice.

The odds the punter accepts when betting on his success to initiate a new, improved equilibrium are, of course, subjective matters of his own conjectures about how the other player plans to respond to any move on his part, and that plan, in turn, depends on what the other player conjectures the first player's plan to be. Common knowledge cannot be assumed. Instead, the players are in a situation of the reflecting mirrors type: "I think that he thinks that I think, etc." Such infinite regress will naturally be stopped quite short if it is to serve any practical purpose and avoid cumulative error. In any case, nothing prejudges its result to be typically dissuasive, and nothing prevents the ideal punter who neither loves nor fears risk, from judging each such situation on what he takes it to be its merits and finding the odds that it seems to offer perfectly acceptable in some cases, though probably not in all.

Let First Mover be a maker of brooches and Second Mover a maker of necklaces. Every day each steals a bauble from the other. First Mover would rather sell his brooches to his legitimate customers than have stolen necklaces he can only sell to a fence, and Second Mover would likewise prefer to have necklaces to sell than stolen brooches. However, they stick to their daily routine of mutual theft. On a Sunday, First Mover refrains from stealing Second Mover's necklace. The latter, however, continues the daily routine and steals the former's brooch. In this disequilibrium, a loss for one and a gain for the other are created. The following Sunday, the same moves are repeated and produce the same result. For Second Mover, the best outcome would be the indefinite iteration of disequilibrium every Sunday; next best would be that he, too, refrains from stealing on Sundays; the worst that First Mover gives up the expensive attempt to lure him into a mutual truce on Sundays, reverts to seven-day stealing, and the old, Pareto-inferior equilibrium is restored. Second Mover must decide how far to push his luck, since persistent seeking of his seemingly best alternative must at some point lose him not only it, but also the second-best alternative of the new equilibrium with the Sunday truce. The First Mover must decide on how many Sundays he will unilaterally refrain from stealing and wait to see whether Second Mover will reciprocate. If neither player miscalculates the odds that attach to alternative moves between rational players in these circumstances, a new, improved equilibrium will have been successfully selected. Further improvements to a full weekend no-theft truce and eventually even to a Pareto-optimal seven-days-a-week respect for property might then become progressively less difficult to attain.

THE PATHBREAKER TO FAIRNESS

When a distribution of good or bad things among a designated set of individuals is fair has never been defined with even tolerable clarity. The best practice in the matter is probably the somewhat cavalier one of saying that fair is what most ordinary people in ordinary speech call fair—though such a solution is both erratic and does too much honor to ordinary speech. It is indeed remarkable how the almost total absence of fairness criteria fails to trouble those who employ the word so frequently with such confidence. The confidence may be justified in some very limited contexts. One of these arises in two—or more—person interactions that provoke approval or condemnation by applying to them such yardsticks as decency and not taking advantage. The present section treats fairness in this narrow but not insignificant sense.

Justice is rooted in rules, ownership, and reciprocal agreement. In its pure form, its rules are spontaneous conventions that are all voluntarily adopted rather than agreed by some and imposed on others by virtue of some rule-making rule. In contrast to justice, fairness is rooted in ethical intuitions that need not be unanimous. Some may profess the intuitions that prevail in average opinion without being guided by them in their actions. It is widely held that fair dealing and the maximization of personal interests in the narrow *homo oeconomicus* mode tend to be in conflict, and that there is no built-in machinery for the enforcement of fair conduct in the same way as the machinery that enforces the rules of justice by the self-defense built into behavioral conventions that punish deviation.

Consider now the hoary parable of slicing the cake fairly. The cake has been baked in heaven and is meant to be divided among a defined number of related people, none of whom has any prior claim to it. The person wielding the knife must have the decency not to favor anyone with a bigger slice than the others, and must not take advantage of his having the knife. This platitudinous form of a basic fairness problem is transformed into one of acute interests in the Ultimatum Game, invented by Werner Gueth and tested by him and others in many cunningly devised experiments. In this game, the Proposer offers to divide an unowned cake fallen from heaven between himself and the Respondent in two slices. If the Respondent accepts the share offered to her, they both get their agreed share, while if she refuses, neither gets anything and the cake is snatched away from them. Ostensibly, the Respondent is better off if she accepts any size of slice down to a paper-thin one than if she refuses it and gets nothing.

If the Proposer's offer is indecently low, the Respondent may indulge herself by punishing him and refuse his offer. It costs her but little to do so. The Proposer can reduce the risk of such punishment by pitching his offer higher and making refusal of it more costly to the Respondent. The higher the offer, the safer it is for the Proposer because the more expensive it is for the Respondent to refuse it. Except if the Proposer plays "maximin" and would rather take a paper-thin, minimal slice than run the least risk of getting nothing, he will at some point find that any further reduction of the risk of getting nothing is not worth any further reduction of his share of the cake. The Proposer can only guess where this point might lie and in experimental play is content to go to what Thomas Schelling (1960: 57) called the "focal point." He offers to share half-and-half, and the Respondent seems content with this. Fairness triumphs.

How this fairly uniform and stable-looking result is achieved is a matter of conjecture. The least interesting of these is to suppose that Proposers are fair-minded, like to play fair, and will play fair even at the cost of getting no more than the "fair" share of the cake. This, of course, is a tautology rather than a real conjecture. In a more interesting one, fairness would figure as an instrument helping to maximize the probability-weighted slice of cake the Proposer can expect to earn by issuing his ultimatum.

The real question then arises: Why does the Proposer expect the Respondent to kick over the tray and send the whole cake to hell if she thinks the Proposer is taking advantage of her? The tautological answer is that unfairness to herself and others makes her indignant and wishful to punish it, therefore she will do what she would rather do and punish it albeit at a cost. The nontautological conjecture is that punishing unfairness is instrumental to maximizing the share of the cake she expects to get. It does so by teaching the Proposer that the greedier his ultimatum, the greater the probability of its being rejected and earning a zero payoff.

Admittedly, for the Respondent's tacit threat to be wholly credible and not a bluff, the game cannot be a pure one-off either played again with the same Proposer, or played by other Proposers with her or with other Respondents linked to one another by shared information. However, it must always be the case to some extent in real-life versions of Ultimatum Games. In feudal times, some "unequal bargains" driven by some lord provoked the exodus of serfs (at some immediate cost to themselves) and must have provided some inducement to other lords to treat their serfs with some degree of humanity. One might impute to the same kind of influence the fact that wages in industrial and mining locations far removed from competitive labor markets were not simply driven down to near-subsistence level.

The long and short of the argument of this section is that in order to explain the prevalence of "fair rather than exploitative" solutions in situations where the dice seem loaded in favor of one of the players, it is not necessary to have recourse to an assumption of love of fairness. This is not to claim that such love may not exist, but simply that we might expect some prominent distributive interactions to have the same result when no such love exists as when it does.

In an imaginary all-encompassing Ultimatum Game, the Respondent who is the very first of all Respondents to refuse an offer that by rights she ought to accept because it is better than nothing, is making a sacrifice in much the same way as all pathbreakers do who make the way easier for all who come after them. At least metaphorically, there has to be a first, and the pathbreaker who assumes the role would presumably prefer to be second if she could count on someone else to go first and break a path. Yet, if it were always preferable to wait for someone else to go first, nobody would go first, nobody could go second, and no path would be made to fairness. The sacrifice of teaching a lesson or breaking a path, like the acceptance of the role of sucker in public goods provision and of first mover in equilibrium selection, is a wager whose odds may not attract everybody but should at any rate attract the number needed to produce gains for themselves and everybody else.

CONCLUSION

If all we can say about people's choices is that they do what they would rather do than anything else available, it is a pointless truism to call all choices selfish. The truism obviously continues to hold when people make manifest sacrifices that benefit other people. They would do these benign things rather than anything else. Perhaps we should say, a little wryly, that they are being selflessly selfish. The behavioral approach to the moral sciences finds it sufficient to attribute this to people liking to advance the interests of other people, wishing to conform to recognized behavioral norms, or seeking approval by others. Pursuing diverse notions of fairness also figures as an end explaining behavior. It is reasonable enough to concede that all these putative ends do influence human conduct, though it is disconcerting to learn that people seek approval because they like to be approved of, or that a sense of solidarity induces them to support a group objective they personally do not much care for. The trouble with such a list of disparate final ends is that, being incommensurate, their combination cannot be maximized. Any combination that is chosen is the best; it cannot be improved or criticized.

This article has taken a close look at three well-known interactions that between them cover an important part of a society's functions: the provision of public goods, the selection and eventually the improvement of coordination equilibria, and the pathbreaking action by which its potential victim discourages the "unfair" division of the proverbial cake. In each, the probability of expected actions by others plays a key part. Such interaction postulates some apparent sacrifice of a player's prima facie interest or dominant strategy; the player appears to be selfless for the purposes of the interaction. It turns out, however, that the selflessness, though the sacrifice it requires is real enough, does not serve the good of others as a final end. The good of others emerges as a by-product, a sort of positive externality. The final end is the good of the player himself. Moreover, his good ("welfare") can at least conceptually be maximized in the neoclassical tradition where *homo oeconomicus* can use what A. C. Pigou (1912: 3) called "the measuring rod of money" to add up his goods. Let at least that part of purposive human action be illuminated by the criteria of rationality. The rest, important as it may be, will have to be left, unfalsifiably, to look after itself.

REFERENCES

Olson, M. (1965) *The Logic of Collective Action.* Cambridge, Mass.: Harvard University Press.

Pigou, A. C. (1912) *Wealth and Welfare.* London: Macmillan.

Shelling, T. (1960) *The Strategy of Conflict.* Cambridge, Mass.: Harvard University Press.

2. WHO WILL GUARD THE GUARDIANS?

With Werner Güth and Hartmut Kliemt

INTRODUCTION

The ancient question of "who guards the guardians" insinuates, in allegorical form, the doubt whether a government can be entrusted with something precious, such as golden eggs or the social order. The doubt persists and divides opinion. The present note was written under the impulse of such a division, namely a debate between Sir Ken Binmore and Anthony de Jasay. Binmore, alluding to the Folk Theorem, pointed out that there can be indefinitely repeated games with subgame perfect equilibria according to which guardians cooperate and prevent deviations by threats of punishment. Jasay objected that since the rule is self-referential, i.e., commands only adherence to itself but neither requires nor allows anything else, the rule and behavior under it is of no interest; logically it is incomplete, while in practice it does not explain why we need guardians at all. We need them to guard something rather than only themselves. In the scenario of the so-called Folk Theorem they seem to be only there to monitor themselves; i.e., they punish deviations from cooperation and they punish each other if they fail to punish each other, etc.

Precisely the same problem under a more general name was brilliantly explored by Herbert Hart in his 1964 essay "Self-referring Laws."[1] Deriving fundamental propositions from Hans Kelsen and John Austin, Hart showed a rule providing only for its own enforcement (e.g., guardians having to force each other to force each other) is empty, and to have any real content needs also to refer to some other requirement. As Hart puts it, ". . . the idea of punishing for a breach of a rule is essentially incomplete. It is incomplete without the idea of a rule which requires behavior other than punishment."[2]

Previously unpublished; reprinted by permission of Anthony de Jasay, Hartmut Kliemt, and Werner Güth.

1. In H. L. A. Hart, *Essays in Jurisprudence and Philosophy* (Oxford: Clarendon, 1983).

2. Ibid., 173.

The game theoretic solution of the problem of social order in terms of "endogenous self-guarding" is backed by strict mathematical proof. This puts its internal validity beyond reasonable doubt. Yet the Folk-Theorem solution of the guardians' problem applies, of course, only under certain conditions. In particular, the circles of threats on which the (subgame perfect) equilibrium strategies of the theorem are based can exist only if the game that is repeated has a certain payoff structure according to which all who are guarding themselves are in a way members of the same circle of mutual interdependence.

In this note we first give a simple informal account of the so-called Hobbesian problem of social order in terms of hierarchical guardianship and its "folk solution." After this we emphasize that it is a contingent empirical rather than a formal issue whether or not the problem of "guarding the guardians" exists and when it conceivably can be solved as outlined by the Folk Theorem(s). Some final observations of a more general nature end our discussion.

THE HOBBESIAN ORDER PROBLEM

Hobbes assumes that all human individuals can and must make their choices according to the anticipated causal consequences of each choice taken separately. Choice makers who are rational in this sense can be bound by (un-)stated rules only to the extent that sanctions render conformity opportunistically rational for them in each and every instance of choice.

In the Hobbesian tradition norms are wishes issued by someone who can inflict sanctions in case of noncompliance. A norm is binding on its addressee to the extent that the addressee believes that a "sufficiently deterrent" sanction will regularly be inflicted by a guardian in cases of deviation.

With this explication of how norms can "bind" rational actors the problem of "who guards the guardians"[3] emerges in the following way:

3. See Juvenal, *Satire* VI. The canonists already commented on the inability of the pope to tie his own hands. The pope cannot constrain his future choices by an act of his own will nor can others do so since he is the highest in the hierarchy of the church.

A. Like the actors whom they supervise, the guardians of the rules of the moral and legal order are choice makers who choose opportunistically rational.
B. Enforcement is a strictly hierarchical process.
C. In the hierarchy of enforcing behavior there must always be at least one (rational) guardian lacking a higher "guardian."
D. From A and B it follows that under "hierarchical guardianship" there must be at least one "unguarded guardian" who makes his choices case by case, without the threat of a sanction by a higher guardian to perform certain acts regularly.

According to conclusion C the ideal of a "government by rules, not men" in which *all* individuals are subject to norms is beyond the reach of a hierarchically organized community of rational individuals. If the "sovereign"[4] is the rational guardian ranking highest in the hierarchy, then by definition he cannot be guarded by a higher guardian. Therefore, the highest guardian cannot be bound to show certain types of behavior by regularly expected sanctions. At the same time the Hobbesian assumption of case by case decision making in view of the causal consequences of each act taken separately rules out that the sovereign guards himself by intrinsically motivated genuine rule following.

In short, the idea of government by rules rather than men, in which all actors are bound by rules, cannot be realized. Since the top dog is of necessity "off the leash," the commitment to rules breaks down at the top. Of course, the ability to threaten need not be asymmetric.

CIRCLES OF GUARDIANS

Imagine a complete circle of guardians: Each guardian shall cut off the head of the one standing in front of him if the latter disobeys the "order" of cutting off the head of the guardian in front of him if the latter disobeys the general "order," etc. When the ring is complete, every guardian has another guardian behind him who will cut off his head if he disobeys.

4. See Jean Bodin, *On Sovereignty* (Cambridge: Cambridge University Press, 1992).

By this construction no hierarchy is necessary, no Red Queen of Hearts. It suffices that each guardian believes that the one behind him will cut off his head if and only if he should disobey and that the belief will never be tested. Each guardian believes in each instance of choice making that he will lose or save his head depending on the strategy choice of the guardian behind him. Disobedience therefore produces at best the same payoff as obedience, and at worst a worse payoff. No sane guardian will disobey.[5]

The preceding circle of threats metaphorically illustrates the kind of equilibrium arguments that eliminate the necessity of assuming the presence of a highest guardian in a hierarchy of threats. Yet the metaphor raises the obvious question whether the argument works if the guardians guard anything beyond themselves.

GUARDIANS AND PEOPLE

The Extractive Herder Game

Imagine an interaction between merely two actors, "sovereign" and "people," concerning the share of eggs laid by people. Assume that between these two players a constant "base game" of "taking or leaving" eggs is repeated indefinitely. Assume also that in the base game of each period it is not in the interest of the guardians to refrain from taking the eggs. Even under repetition it does not make sense for the guardians to keep from mistreating the people since "people" cannot sanction—threaten or reward—(sovereign) guardians.

This boils down to the assumption that "sovereign" and "people," though part of the same game, are "not in the same circle." "Sovereign" can inflict costly consequences on "people" at no cost to herself. This is the limiting case of the cost asymmetries that characterize political

5. The behavior of players of a repeated game contains actions that are interpreted as "punishment" or "reward." Both types of moves in base games are part of the supergame strategies of the players. The supergame strategies contain a response for any contingency that may show up in the course of a play of the game (the strategies specify fully the actions of the actor for any choice situation in the game). Such strategies are in sequential equilibrium if in all choice situations no individual can do better against the strategies of all others.

power and constitute what it means to be "hierarchically superior" in political relationships.[6]

To give a specific illustration of the preceding setup, think of the game as one of "herding geese." The geese lay two "golden eggs" in each period no matter what. Let a base game like the following be repeated indefinitely for t = 1, 2, . . . :

TABLE 1

		Column = "people"	
		"left"	"right"
Row = "sovereign"	"Take" (away eggs)	1, 1	1, 1
	"Leave" (eggs alone)	0, 2	0, 2

Clearly "sovereign" will "take" on each round of play of this specific herding game. "People" cannot make a strategically relevant choice. They are production automata laying their eggs no matter what. Whether they choose "left" or "right" does not affect any payoffs—neither their own nor those of the "sovereign." There is nothing to gain for the "sovereign" by behavior other than playing the strictly dominant strategy of the base game on each round of its repetition. Only if we alter the assumptions about the base game of table 1 can "sovereign" and "people" become members of the same circle of strategic interdependence.

The Nonextractive Herding Game

In the metaphorical world of eggs, geese, and guardians, imagine that the geese can reduce their production of eggs in the future if they do not receive a "sufficient" share of the eggs "in the present." If the geese can in this or some other way affect the payoffs of the guardians in response to actions of the guardians, they are not mere dummies in the game but become strategic players. "People" can themselves guard the guardians who guard them.[7]

6. An individual is hierarchically superior if she can inflict relatively higher costs on another individual at relatively lower costs to herself (both measured according to quotients of differences on their own utility functions).

7. To render the relevant equilibrium behavior subgame perfect the guardians

More specifically, assume that the payoff structure of the "guardian" and "people" interaction is such that on each round of play a standard prisoner's dilemma emerges.

TABLE 2

		Column = "people"	
		"left"	"right"
Row = "sovereign"	Exploit	2, 2	4, 1
	Protect	1, 4	3, 3

In the base game corresponding to the preceding table "people" can respond to "takings" by "guardian(s)" with reduced production activity. Therefore, if as corporate actors "guardian" and "people" form a circle in which they influence each other strategically in the appropriate way according to their supergame strategies, "people" can guard the "guardian" who guards the "people" and the standard circular solution of the problem of "who guards the guardian(s)" applies.

In sum, in the extractive herder as well as in the nonextractive herder game the "guardian problem" vanishes. If payoffs are as in table 1, there is obviously no way to guard the guardians. As long as "ought" presupposes "can" no solution needs to be sought. If the payoff structure of table 2 prevails, "guardian" can be controlled by "people" and vice versa. Again the problem of who guards the guardians ceases to exist.

Looking "into" the Corporate Guardian

The preceding solution of the guardian problem does not crucially depend on "people" and "guardian" acting as unitary actors or single players. To illustrate, in table 3 below it is assumed that the collective payoff is shared by guardian i, $i = 1, 2$:

must punish people for not punishing them and people must punish them for not punishing, etc. The Folk Theorem shows in its refined version that such subgame perfect equilibria exist.

TABLE 3 *Guarding the Golden Eggs Game*

		People					
		Produce eggs P_3				Not produce eggs N_3	
		Guardian 2				Guardian 2	
		T_2	L_2			T_2	L_2
Guardian 1	T_1	$(1, 1, -c)$	$(2, 0, -c)$	Guardian 1	T_1	$(0, 0, 0)$	$(0, 0, 0)$
	L_1	$(0, 2, -c)$	$(0, 0, 2-c)$		L_1	$(0, 0, 0)$	$(0, 0, 0)$

($1 > c > 0$, $L_i \approx$ "Leave," $T_i \approx$ "Take," $i = 1, 2$)

In the game of table 3 the individual guardian players have each a weakly dominant strategy of taking. If the combination (T_1, T_2) of these strategies is used, then the best response of "people" is not to produce eggs, N_3. The base game represented in table 3 therefore has a unique (perfect) equilibrium (T_1, T_2, N_3). This equilibrium will yield (0, 0, 0).

All players could gain in equilibrium by some combination of supergame strategies leading on average to a convex combination of $(1, 1, -c)$ and $(0, 0, 2 - c)$ such that all components of $\Delta(1, 1, -c) + (1 - \Delta)(0, 0, 2 - c)$ are positive. According to the Folk Theorem there are perfect equilibria in supergame strategies that yield (L_1, L_2, P_3) base game choice profiles in some of the periods.[8] That is, the two, "guardian 1" and "guardian 2," have an interest now not to take it all in each period. Contingent strategies according to which guardian i sanctions guardian j, $i \neq j$, indirectly through the sanctioning supergame strategy of player 3 would become viable. For instance, if player 3 can only choose among completely mixed strategies then guardians can punish each other. The emerging equilibria are not stationary and therefore do not represent the most simple form of an order.

ARE THERE NONEXTRACTIVE GOVERNMENT GAMES?

Imagine a group of herdsmen who herd commonly owned geese to get as many eggs as possible. Then the "herd" should be well kept and fed.

8. For instance, one could think of so-called grim strategies here: each player will sanction any deviation from the joint randomization envisioned by eternal deviation.

Therefore, in the game between guarded herd and guarding herdsmen no problem of guarding the guardians need to arise. If treating the herd badly would negatively affect the interests of the herdsmen and vice versa, the standard equilibrium argument would do.

One should be aware, however, of the fact that the collective good of the guardians—the size of their collective pie—must depend on people in ways the guardians cannot control. If the latter is not the case, then the game of table 1 rather than the game of table 2 will emerge and the government will become entirely extractive. The authors of this paper are themselves not of one opinion on how likely the dismal prospects of government are. They agree, though, that the risk that government becomes completely extractive is always there.

The British Moralists, in particular Hume, concurred. But they emphasized that there might be incentives for a "guardian" to adopt the role of a "herdsman" rather than acting as an extracting "hunter-gatherer." "Guardian" might have an incentive to see to it that his flock, the "people," would produce goods—golden eggs—that "guardian" could then at least in part extract as rents.

As long as "people" can, say, "go slow" or respond to "guardian's" actions in ways that would affect the payoffs of "guardian," the Folk Theorem could do its work and keep "guardian" from becoming too extractive. "Guardian" would have to take into account the reactions of "people" to the extent that "people" are (other than in the game of table 1) a relevant strategic player. To *the extent* that this is *in fact* true there is indeed no problem of "who guards the guardians?"; "people" and "guardian" guard themselves in equilibrium.

If, however, the "guardian" is a dictator in the full sense, exemplified by the payoff structure of a "dictator game"—and for that matter by table 1—then the Folk Theorem would not apply to the external interaction between "guardian" and "people," and a fortiori looking into the box of "guardian" as corporate actor would not help at all. The guardians would indeed have nothing to guard; they could take everything anyway with indemnity. No Folk Theorem could help that. Again the problem of who guards the guardians would vanish, though now for the worse.

It seems a largely empirical issue whether and to what extent real world guardians have to take into account responses by the guarded. If the guarded can respond in ways that are affecting the guardian group negatively, then all guardians of that group would have an incentive to play in equilibrium in ways that do not require other guardians to adopt a special role to make fellow guardians behave adequately.

In his treatment of government Hume saw a problem here still. Individual guardians may need to control the human preference for what is close and tempting in their fellow guardians. Folk Theorems under so-called "hyperbolic discounting" can capture this but, to keep this note reasonably short, will not be discussed here.[9]

REFERENCES

Bodin, J. *On Sovereignty.* Cambridge: Cambridge University Press.

Hart, H. L. A. *Essays in Jurisprudence and Philosphy.* Oxford: Clarendon Press.

9. The greatness of Hume is that he was always a theorist of bounded rather than of full or perfect rationality. Unlike many later psychological theories, Hume's psychological theory stresses the rational in the bounded rationality concept.

3. CAN OPPORTUNITY BE EQUAL? A NOTE ON FALSE PRETENSES IN EQUALITY DISCOURSE

The main body of egalitarian thought and sentiment is concerned with divisible and transferable claims to goods and services and postulates that the possession and consumption of these goods should be distributed among eligible individuals in equal parts. The postulate is either deemed to be self-evident and requiring no supporting argument, or claimed to be supported by one of two arguments. One is metaphysical and seeks to establish that individuals have moral dispositions, such as the sense of fairness, the sense of empathy, and the dread of risk, that induce them to value equal distributions of given aggregates of goods more highly than unequal ones even if the unequal one favored their immediate material interest. The other supporting argument refers to man's prehistoric manner of life in which an equal distribution of food was a better evolutionary selector for genetic survival than retention of the food in unequal parts by the individual who first acquired it by hunting and gathering. The genes of present-day mankind continue to predispose it to egalitarian distribution regardless of whether the latter is still the best survival strategy.

These arguments are contentious, and egalitarian thought is correspondingly controversial in the academy, while on politics it is a source of acrimony for reasons both of conviction and of personal and class interest. However, hovering on the margins of the central bulk of egalitarian theory, there are a number of ersatz ideas, less demanding, less threatening to the personal interests of the better-off and easily accepted by general opinion, that yet retain some of the emotional appeal of the language of equality. This note will touch upon three of these ideas. In increasing order of influence, they are equal treatment, equality before the law, and equal opportunity. Only the last of these

Previously unpublished; © 2015 by Liberty Fund, Inc.

three will be discussed here in any detail. All three will prove to be carrying the word "equal" in their names with little justification and to misleading effect.

"Equal treatment" is widely agreed to be a defining feature of a well-ordered society. The statement is uncontested because it is a direct derivative of the uncontested axiom that like cases must be treated alike. However, no two cases are alike in all respects, for if they were not unlike in at least one respect, they would not be two cases. Two cases can be treated alike in one respect. As an inevitable consequence, they will be treated unlike in at least one other respect, and very likely in many more than one. Two individuals, both salaried employees, are given pension rights proportional to their formal salary and exercisable at age sixty-five. This is equal treatment of the two. One is a man, the other a woman, and their life expectancy differs by five years; hence their treatments are unequal and favor the woman. Raising the woman's contribution above those of the man's to allow for her longer life expectancy would be to treat her unequally. No treatment of the two can be devised that, equal in some respects, would not be unequal in others. Calling any one of the equal respects "equal treatment" is a misnomer, even if we judged the equal treatments accorded to the two individuals rather than the unequal ones.

"Equality before the law!" is a notion needing clarification. Imagine a law providing that "commoners must not steal." By implication and omission, nobles may. (For nobles, you may substitute the wealthy and the well connected.) Commoners are equal before the law, being convicted and sentenced if found guilty of stealing. Nobles are also equal before the law, and are left free to steal. It makes sense to complain that this law is unjust, but it is nonsense to complain that there is no equality before the law. The division of a population into two classes, nobles and commoners, is of course provocative and may raise our hackles. However, many other divisions into classes are readily accepted as serving useful purposes in a legal order. Nobody calls for equality before the law when criminal law treats adults differently from juvenile defendants. Any number of other examples may be found where different laws apply to different classes of a population. One may not call all of them judicious, but it is a misnomer to call one's objection an appeal to equality before the law. On the other hand, if in the face of a law providing that "nobody must steal" a commoner thief is convicted but a noble thief is acquitted on some technicality or sentenced more leniently than the commoner, it is proper usage to invoke the equality-before-the-law principle. However, the principle is not a derivative of the broad principle of equality. Instead, it is merely a corollary of the commonsense proposition that if you are subject to a law, your compliance to it is mandatory.

Equality of opportunity may well be a sort of ersatz equality and in that capacity may resemble equal treatment and equality before the law. However, it is both more demanding and plays a very particular role in the attempt to reconcile the integrity of property and contract with egalitarianism. The formula employed to this effect is that moderate egalitarianism "does not require equality of outcomes, but is satisfied with equality of opportunities." This placatory claim is false, though it is probably not knowingly made to mislead.

"To have an opportunity" may be defined as being in a position associated with a nonzero (or, less stringently, a nonnegligible) probability of its being enriched with a significant reward in the foreseeable future. "Significant" is meant to describe a reward that is valued by the recipient a good deal more highly than the average run of benefits he reaps in the ordinary course of his life. The significant reward in effect practically changes the course of his life. Two kinds of such exceptional rewards should be distinguished according to their source. One, that we may call "controlled," is deliberately generated by a controller and is awarded primarily so as to serve the latter's purposes. An example is the corporation that creates a rewarding job vacancy in its organization and fills it with a candidate chosen from a number of applicants according to how well qualified he seems to be for the job. The other kind of reward, which might be called "natural," offers itself to the individual on a probabilistic basis spontaneously as an exceptional item occurring in the course of events that constitute his life. Evidently, some types of life are liable to be punctuated by more opportunities for exceptional rewards than others. Not all of these are job opportunities; they may involve new and interesting sets of friends and fruitful business deals, as well as (for men) getting to know attractive women and (for women) meeting and attracting men of good looks and character who are likely to be good providers. Such differentials would be over and above those that could simply be ascribed to Fortune's wheel.

An opportunity to earn a controlled reward in the above example has a probability that varies with the candidate's qualifications for the job and the qualifications of rival candidates. Let us suppose, absurdly simplified, that the sole qualification required is that the candidate must have a Ph.D. and nobody else wanting the job has one. His opportunity then is rewarded with probability 1—i.e., he gets the job—while the probability of anyone else getting it is 0. For equal opportunity, everybody must be enabled to get a Ph.D. At the time of writing this note, the compulsory schooling age ends as early as sixteen or eighteen years. Believing as we do in progress, we may expect that before long compulsory education will be prolonged until everybody secures a Ph.D. All will then have equal opportunity with near-zero probability of a reward. Before this happens, however, the opportunity controller will have changed the qualification needed to compete for the rewarding job from a single Ph.D. to two or three Ph.D.s—in fact, to as many as it takes to restore it as a selection device. Everybody with one Ph.D. will have equality and practically no opportunity. Having more Ph.D.s than most other people will, in turn, mean inequality but opportunity to have a reasonable probability of being rewarded.

A fundamentally analogous mechanism lowers the probability of people catching the natural rewards that cross their life path as the proportion of persons having rich, varied, interesting lives rises. Children with parents who have influential friends and young people with friends made at elite schools, near the center of large and useful networks, will come across more naturally occurring rewards and fewer rivals with opportunities if most young people do not have the advantages they do. The advantages can perhaps be spread more widely and stretched flatter by levelling down all the parents and all the schools and making access to clubs free for all, but as and when this is done, the probability of opportunities producing actual rewards will fall pari passu because of more and more competitors entering the race for them. In the limit, opportunities would become worthless as they became equal.

The progressive social philosopher Ronald Dworkin has further enhanced his already great popularity by launching the formula that the egalitarian goal should be "equality at the starting gate," and not of end states, a goal smelling of the fresh and free air of competition and emancipated from the coercive odium of redistribution. This seemingly harmless prescription fails to make it clear that before the horses are placed on the same line they have to be conveyed there from the wildly unequal positions they occupy outside the racecourse. Conveying them to the starting gate and lining them up is tantamount to equalizing the end state of the horses' existence before they start racing. They have to be ridden to the starting gate from somewhere else, each from a different stable, from different lives in which they have not been level with each other. Without equalizing the preceding end state, there can be no equality at the starting gate. How anyone, let alone Dworkin's whole audience, could fail to see this is difficult to fathom. The attractive horsey metaphor should not hide it that a necessary condition of equality of opportunity is equality of an end state.

4. MORALS BY AGREEMENTS

Gauthier's theory of a social order that is also moral seems to me to be grounded on two major conceptual errors. They vitiate much of his superstructure and are also partly the cause of its being inordinately complicated, tortuous, and turgid. The present comment will focus on what I claim to be the foundational errors.

CONSTRAINED MAXIMIZATION

This is a pleonasm like "white snow." If unconstrained maximization were a sensible idea, it could make sense only under the exceptional condition of Robinson Crusoe playing by himself before he becomes aware of Man Friday; and even then, his game would be a game against Nature and his strategy would have to take account of Nature's probable best response to it. In normal human society, the expected payoff is maximized if it allows for the effect upon it of the expected best responses of the other game participants. If no such allowance is made, the chosen strategy is not a maximizing strategy. The claim of Gauthier that his "constrained" maximization is different from common and garden maximization is a howler, and that it is a stepping stone to morality is futile.

Compared to this foundational fault, the failure to admit that solutions that apply to repeated games do not logically apply to the one-off prisoner's dilemma is only a minor blemish, but it is disturbing.

AGREEMENT

If in the state of nature a driver chooses to drive on the right because he is meeting fewer vehicles head-on than he would if he chose to drive on the left, he does not do so "by agreement." There is no agreement, overt or tacit. Instead, there is unilateral adhesion to a strategy that

Previously unpublished; © 2015 by Liberty Fund, Inc.

looks more advantageous than its rival(s). The emergence of the corresponding conventional rule of the road may be "modelled" as instantaneous or as the slow result of evolutionary biology. Occam's razor would cut off as unnecessary the hypothesis that the convention results from agreement.

Compare the two ways of arriving at the convention against stealing. In the initial situation I steal from my neighbor every day and he steals from me every day. As First Mover, I refrain from stealing one day of the week in the hope that he as Second Mover will reciprocate, but I take the risk that he will not. If he did, a convention of stealing only on six days a week might emerge. Five-day, four-day, etc., conventions might or might not succeed it, and the nonstealing Pareto optimum is also possible. The Folk Theorem proves that each alternative is a possible equilibrium.

If Gauthier's insistence on agreement is more than rhetoric, it seems to imply that before moving, First Mover asks Second Mover how he would respond to his nonstealing move, and Second Mover invariably responds that he would reciprocate. First Mover believes this and moves accordingly. (Note that First Mover must take a risk in either scenario. Note also that the first modus operandi belongs to noncooperative, the second to cooperative game theory.)

In calling his agreement-based social order "contractarian," Gauthier seems to conflate two distinct concepts, agreement and contract. In the contract, each party assumes an obligation to do something he would not do if he had not undertaken to do it; the obligation is incurred because it is the price of the other party obliging himself to do what he would otherwise not do. If performance is sequential, once First Performer has discharged his obligation, Second Performer's best response is to default. This may well not be the case if the contract is iterated, but not every contract is iterated. It can be a one-shot game. By contrast, a convention is by definition an indefinite series of iterated games which, being equilibria, have cooperation as each player's best response to the other's cooperation. The upshot is that a system of conventions is an order in which every participant is doing what he wishes to do and not what he has contracted to do. To say that each participant agrees to do what he wishes to do sounds silly and I think it is. Calling such an order contractarian seems to be a misnomer. Note that in the two most representative contractarian theories, the desired result, namely some qualified equality of goods, is obtained by a special assumption (in Buchanan the veil of uncertainty, in Rawls the veil of ignorance) in such a way that players' choice is unanimous. They all do what they wish to do; prior agreement, let alone contract, is redundant.

SOME CONSEQUENCES

If conventions are spontaneous coordination equilibria producing advantages for all participants—*which I believe is the best theoretical conception we have of them*—then the advantages to each are determined by the features describing the interaction. When the stronger boy defends the weaker one in the school yard, the former gains prestige and self-esteem, and the latter is spared hard knocks.

However, when the conventional conduct is the result of prior agreement between the cooperating players, as it is in Gauthier, it is not implausible to suppose that some bargain over the division of the game sum, i.e., the total advantage, may form part of the agreement. In fact, nothing seems to stop us from postulating that without the parties managing to reach a bargain, there will be no agreement to cooperate. Nor will it be easy to resist the widely gaping opportunity to theorize about what the bargain ought to look like in order to be justifiable and help to constitute a moral order.

Thus, the supposition that conventional rules of conduct are the product of agreement seems to be at the origin of Gauthier's regrettable ambition to derive conditions such bargains ought to conform to in order to be moral. Without mandatory bargaining, and without the "minimum relative concession" the bargaining must have as its mandatory issue, the whole theory of morals by agreement would be less tortured and less easy to dismiss.

One might add, for good measure, that even if all conduct were the result of agreement, the advantages accruing to each participant would usually be incommensurate, raising the notorious controversies about interpersonal comparisons. Total advantages may also be indivisible.

INDEX

The typeface used for this book is ITC New Baskerville,
which was created for the International Typeface Corporation and is
based on the types of the English type founder and printer John Baskerville
(1706–75). Baskerville is the quintessential transitional face: it retains the
bracketed and oblique serifs of old-style faces such as Caslon and Garamond,
but in its increased lowercase height, lighter color, and enhanced contrast
between thick and thin strokes it presages modern faces.

The display type is set in Adobe Walbaum.

Printed on paper that is acid-free and meets the requirements
of the American National Standard for Permanence of Paper for
Printed Library Materials, z39.48-1992. ♾

Book design by Richard Hendel, Chapel Hill, North Carolina

Typography by Tseng Information Systems, Inc., Durham, North Carolina

Printed and bound by Worzalla Publishing Company,
Stevens Point, Wisconsin